BY THE SAME AUTHOR

FELONY FILE   SCHOOLED TO KILL
FELONY AT RANDOM   KILL WITH KINDNESS
COLD TRAIL   RAIN WITH VIOLENCE
APPEARANCES OF DEATH   CHANCE TO KILL
STREETS OF DEATH   WITH A VENGEANCE
CRIME FILE   COFFIN CORNER
DEUCES WILD   DEATH BY INCHES
SPRING OF VIOLENCE   THE DEATH-BRINGERS
NO HOLIDAY FOR CRIME   MARK OF MURDER
WITH INTENT TO KILL   ROOT OF ALL EVIL
MURDER WITH LOVE   DOUBLE BLUFF
THE RINGER   DEATH OF A BUSYBODY
WHIM TO KILL   KNAVE OF HEARTS
UNEXPECTED DEATH   EXTRA KILL
CRIME ON THEIR HANDS   THE ACE OF SPADES
CASE PENDING

MURDER
MOST
STRANGE

Dell Shannon

WILLIAM MORROW AND COMPANY, INC.

New York   1981

Library of Congress Cataloging in Publication Data

Linington, Elizabeth.
  Murder most strange.

  I. Title.
PS3562.I515M8   813'.54   80-24573
ISBN 0-688-00378-8

Printed in the United States of America

First Edition
1   2   3   4   5   6   7   8   9   10

This one is for

MARTHA WEBB
a real-life cop
who likes my cops

Of all the ways of defining man, the worst is the one which makes him out to be a rational animal.

—ANATOLE FRANCE

MURDER
MOST
STRANGE

ONE

The elevator door slid back silently on the long hospital corridor. Just opposite was the L-shaped desk in a bay of a nurses' station, and a tall blond young fellow in white smock and pants was lounging there casually talking to half a dozen nurses; apparently he'd just gotten to the punch line of a joke, and they were all laughing as Mendoza and Hackett came up.

"Dr. O'Laughlin," said Hackett, "called to say—"

"Me." He surveyed them; he looked too young to be anything but an intern. "You'll be the fuzz."

"Lieutenant Mendoza, Sergeant Hackett."

"Yep," said O'Laughlin. "Down this way. She was damned lucky, he just missed the heart with one blow, and she'd lost a hell of a lot of blood. Yeah, she's been conscious since about four A.M., but you can only see her for ten minutes or so— she's still weak, so take it easy." He looked at them interestedly, Mendoza as usual dapper in silver-gray herringbone, Hackett looming bulkily over him. Halfway down the hall he stopped at a door. This was the Intensive Care section of the huge sprawling pile of Cedars–Sinai Medical Center: beyond the window to their left was a rather spectacular view, from five storeys up, out over Hollywood.

In the two-bed room, the second bed had curtains drawn around it, the occupant invisible; in the bed nearest the door, Cindy Hamilton was half propped up against pillows, an I.V. tube in one arm. Her dark hair was brushed lankly back from her pale face, and she looked disappointed to see the three men; her mouth drooped.

"I thought—Mother'd be back."

"Later," said O'Laughlin easily. "You're off the critical list now, darling, and visitors' hours haven't begun yet. It's the police with some questions, Cindy—we do want to catch the fellow who did this, don't we?"

"Oh," she said. "Oh, yes." She looked at Mendoza and Hackett with faint interest. "Only I haven't the least idea who he was, you know."

"Can you give us a description of him?" asked Hackett, getting out his notebook.

"Oh, my God," said Cindy Hamilton, and shut her eyes briefly. They knew quite a bit about her now, and she was a nice girl. She was twenty-five, and she had a job as a legal secretary, one of three girls in the office of Daniel Frome on Beverly Boulevard; she lived alone in an apartment on Hoover. Her original home was Fallbrook, where she still had family; her parents were here now. Three days ago, last Monday, she hadn't showed up at work, and eventually one of the other girls had gone to the apartment, as they couldn't raise her on the phone, and discovered the door open and Cindy unconscious and bloody on the living-room floor. She'd been beaten, stabbed and raped.

"My God," she said again now. "Yes, I can do that all right." She was obviously still weak, but she tried to pull herself up straighter in the bed and raised a hand to smooth her hair. "Gah. I feel like death warmed over. Mother and Dad at me to come home to Fallbrook, the big city so dangerous. You know, I'm sort of thinking about it now. And you'll think I'm a fool—but you just don't know—how—how *damned* plausible he was! It—he—" She shook her head. "It was just like Jekyll and Hyde."

"How do you mean, Miss Hamilton?" asked Hackett.

"Funny isn't the right word. Naturally I'm not idiot enough to let a strange man in—you know, the ordinary way. I've lived in L.A. for three years, I know about the crime rate, for heaven's sake. But he was so nice—so polite. He was—well, a gentleman, you know?" She drew a long breath. "I'll tell you —all I can, if it'll help to catch him. It was about four o'clock on Sunday afternoon, the doorbell rang and there he was. Never saw him before, but he looked—" She thought, and decided on, "Nice. Nobody to be afraid of. He was about twenty-five or thirty, tall, around six feet, dark hair, clean shaven, sort of thin—and dressed real sharp, a gray suit, not just sports clothes, a whole suit, white shirt and tie. I mean, he looked—oh, like a professional man of some kind, certainly not a bum or a dopey—and he was so polite." She swallowed. "That was why. Why I was such a fool to let him in. Because —it sounded—he made it sound so plausible."

"What, Miss Hamilton?" asked Hackett.

Her eyes moved over the three of them listening, closed again. "Such a *fool*," she said. "He said—he was looking for his sister. He thought she lived there, at my apartment, I mean —he'd had a letter and they were supposed to have moved there last week, his sister and her husband—he took out a letter from his pocket to check the address. He said a name— something like Wayne or Raynes, I don't remember. And he'd just gotten to L.A. from someplace back East, he couldn't understand why they weren't here. He sounded—he looked so really upset and worried. And I said I didn't know anything about it, of course, and he thanked me—he seemed just terribly worried, and he apologized—and then he said he'd sent his taxi away because he'd expected to find his sister there, and he supposed he'd have to go to their old address and see if they were there, and did I mind if he called another taxi—"

"*Ca*," said Mendoza interestedly.

"And like an absolute fool I let him in. Like Jekyll and

15

Hyde," said Cindy Hamilton weakly. "As soon as—the door was shut—he whipped out his knife, and he was on me—didn't give me time to scream—all of a sudden, he looked just like a fiend, this awful fixed grin, and he—and he—"

"Can you tell us anything more about his appearance? Color of eyes? Any scars or tattoos?"

She shook her head. "It was all sort of fast, after that. Feel like such a fool. But he was so plausible—" Her eyes shut again.

"That'll do for now," said O'Laughlin. In the corridor, he was disposed to ask curious questions, but Hackett was curt and he shrugged and took himself off.

"And that's something a little different, isn't it?" said Hackett. "She might be able to make a mug shot."

Mendoza was teetering back and forth, heel to toe, ruminatively. "It rings a small bell in my head," he said.

"What? An offbeat sort of thing—"

"Mmh. Come on, Arturo, let's go back to base and chase it up."

They had driven over in Hackett's garish Monte Carlo; it was early afternoon and the traffic light. In twenty minutes they were back at Parker Center downtown, and came into the Robbery-Homicide office to find Landers and Palliser just leaving on a new call. "Probably not much," said Sergeant Lake pithily. "Body over on Miramar. Patrolman said looked like a typical old wino."

Mendoza swept off the inevitable black Homburg and started for his office. "Get me Hollywood, Jimmy—Sergeant Barth if he's in." He sat down at his desk and swiveled around to stare out at the view toward the Hollywood hills over the urban complex sprawl of downtown L.A. It was a clear view, this last day of March; the winter months had been wet, and as yet there hadn't been anything like a heat wave or high smog. So far it was a pleasant, cool spring, and Robbery-Homicide was perking along with enough to do, but not as heavy a caseload as they sometimes had to work. They had, of course, the usual heist jobs, and three of those over the last couple of weeks had apparently been pulled by the same pair; they had a shapeless sort of homicide, a derelict wino stabbed to death over on Skid Row, which would probably end up in Pending. There was a still unidentified body which had turned up three days ago in a cheap hotel room: an O.D. on heroin, the autopsy said, and it wouldn't make much difference if they never found out who he'd been. As the year advanced and the inevitable heat wave arrived, business would pick up; at the moment they were out hunting heisters, and cleaning up a rather messy but obvious homicide involving an addict and his supplier—but more business was always coming along.

The phone shrilled on Mendoza's desk and he picked it up. "What do you want?" asked Sergeant Barth of the Hollywood precinct. "I'm busy."

"Just before Christmas," said Mendoza, "I ran into you down in R. and I. with a witness to look at mug shots, and you were telling me something about a gentlemanly rapist. Who talked his way into victims' apartments all very polite and then pulled a knife."

"Dapper Dan," said Barth instantly. "Yeah. Don't tell me you've got something on that one? As far as we know, he pulled seven rapes up here in the last six months, and one turned into a homicide. What's your interest?"

"It's possible we've got another victim in our territory. I'd like to hear what you turned up on it. Didn't you say he had some plausible story about thinking his sister lived at this address, and did the lady mind if he called a cab—"

"That's him," said Barth. "For God's sake. The last we heard of him was in January."

"Come to Papa, please," said Mendoza gently, "with everything you collected. It looks as if he's branched out into new terrain."

"Damn it, I've got a couple of witnesses in to make statements. I'll get down as soon as I can. And hell, Bosworth worked that homicide mostly and it's his day off—I'll be down, I'll be down," said Barth resignedly.

"An offbeat one, all right," said Hackett. "Just chance, you running into Barth like that." But of course, as they went on to work it, NCIC would have pinned down the M.O. and sent them to Hollywood precinct eventually.

Mendoza sat back, lit a cigarette and yawned. "I think I'm coming down with spring fever. Offbeat—I don't know, Art, nothing a rapist does should surprise us, ¿como no?"

There wasn't anyone else in the office. They were short one man on day watch now; it was apparent that the brass wasn't about to assign any new men to the bureau, and instead had transferred Rich Conway to beef up the night watch. They were about to lose Nick Galeano, if temporarily. After more than a year of pussyfooting around his very proper and respectable young German widow, Marta Fleming, he had finally screwed up the courage to propose to her, and the formal wedding was scheduled for next Monday afternoon. Galeano had six days of unused sick leave as well as his vacation coming, and it was just to be hoped that the case load at Robbery-Homicide didn't start to get hot and heavy before he got back to them.

"I've got that report to finish," said Hackett, and reluctantly went back to his desk in the communal office. Most of the heists were, as usual, entirely anonymous with few leads to offer, and he felt rather like coming down with spring fever himself.

Before Barth showed up John Palliser and Tom Landers came back, with the new one to start a report on.

"That old wino, Leo Marvin," said Palliser, absently stroking his handsome straight nose. "About ten days ago—in an alley over on Alameda. Stabbed. It looked a little funny, because he didn't have much on him for anybody to steal, and for a couple of days he'd been too broke even to buy the cheapest stuff—panhandling up on Broadway, said a couple of his pals, and no luck. Why the hell should anybody knife one like that?"

"Annoyed because he didn't have much on him," said Hackett. "What about him?"

"Well, this new body looks sort of like a replay," said Palliser. "It's funny."

Landers tendered a quarter and tossed it. "Heads." Palliser said "Tails" uninterestedly and they looked at it. "Hell," said Landers, and took the cover off his typewriter.

"What do you mean, a replay?" asked Hackett. Mendoza had come wandering out of his office and perched a hip on the corner of Higgins' desk.

"Well, in a way, just such another one," said Palliser. "Except that he wasn't a wino. One Joseph Kelly, retired railroad man, lived on a little pension and Social Security, an old apartment on Miramar. Harmless old widower, no family, evidently not many friends. The man who lives across the hall found him a couple of hours ago, in the hall right outside his apartment door. Stabbed to death, it looks like. And not very long before, he was still warm. And he had about nine bucks on him, so he wasn't robbed either."

"The city jungle," said Mendoza, and yawned again.

"Yes, but—it just struck me as funny," said Palliser. Landers had rolled the triplicate forms into the typewriter and was starting the report.

George Higgins came in towing a weedy, very black young Negro and said, "Good, somebody's here. I finally caught up with Willy." Three witnesses had fingered Willy Lamb for the knifing of another unsavory character who had been supplying him with heroin. "Who'd like to sit in and talk to him?" Higgins looked tired; he'd been out all day following up the few elusive leads to Willy, and probably hadn't had any lunch.

"Oh, stash him away and take a breather," said Mendoza. "You look a little beat, boy."

"I could use a sandwich and coffee, but we ought to get to him while he's still surprised he got tabbed for it." Higgins shepherded his capture out toward one of the interrogation rooms, and Palliser swore and followed him. Quite a lot of the time this was a very boring, dull and sordid job.

19

Landers had finished the report, and it was getting on for four o'clock, when Sergeant Barth of the Hollywood precinct came in. Higgins and Palliser were still closeted with Willy Lamb. Hackett went down the hall to the coffee machine and brought back three cups to Mendoza's office, remembering that Barth liked sugar.

"Thanks very much," said Barth, looking slightly less sour. "My God, what a day—we're in a hell of a mess up on my beat, four homicides this week—four, I ask you—I can remember when Hollywood was the cream-puff beat, and now all these goddamned hookers and pimps cluttering the streets, not to mention the nest of fags— Augh!" He took a swallow of coffee and sighed. He had a year to go to retirement; he'd put in thirty-five years at the job, and today looked his age and more, a middle-sized nondescript fellow with a comfortable little paunch and a nearly bald head. He had laid a fat manila folder on Mendoza's desk, and nodded at it. "There's all we've got on Dapper Dan. You think he's pulled one down here?"

"It sounds suggestive," said Mendoza. "Tell us the highlights."

Barth shrugged. "Seven cases, roughly last September to February. He must have cased the girls at least desultorily, to know they were living alone. But of course they all had their names in the slots in the apartment doors. He gave them all the same story, and they all—that is, except the one who turned up dead—said the same thing. He was so polite, such a gentleman, they didn't hesitate to let him in when he asked. And none of them was the kind who'd admit a strange man in the ordinary way, so he must be damned plausible. The same little tale, and it was just simple enough to sound plausible, I suppose. He'd just landed here from somewhere back East, and this was the new address he had from his sister and her husband, and he was all mystified at finding they weren't there. He padded it out, and every one of the girls believed him—all so apologetic, so sorry to bother them. And they gave us a good description. Five ten to six feet, thin, dark hair, probably dark eyes, clean shaven and very well dressed. Which seems to have been one of the things that reassured them, you see? The natty suit, the white shirt and tie."

"Mmh, yes," said Mendoza. "Not a bum or an addict. What about the homicide?"

"Well, it's very probable it was him," said Barth. "It looked like a carbon copy. In all the other cases, as soon as he got into the apartment he pulled the knife and seemed to go berserk—"

"Jekyll and Hyde," said Hackett.

"Yeah, one of them said that. He only went for the straight rape, nothing kinky, but he was rough—all of them were beaten up and stabbed, two of them seriously. The homicide —well," said Barth, "a hell of a lot of suggestive evidence ties it up to him. Girl named Gay Spencer, lived in an apartment on Fountain. She was a salesclerk at Magnin's. Girl friend of hers worked there too, so when she didn't turn up for work one Monday the girl friend went to see why, found the door unlocked and Spencer dead on the living-room floor. She'd been stabbed twenty-three times, died of shock and blood loss. The autopsy said about twenty-four hours before. That linked it up right there—the knife, and the day—all the jobs were pulled on Sunday afternoons. So we asked around, and two women had seen a man coming up the hall, from the direction of Spencer's apartment, about four o'clock the afternoon before. Same description, if not quite as much of it."

"Yes," said Mendoza. "All on Sundays? That's a queer one."

"Day when a lot of single young girls would be home," said Barth. "Washing their hair or stockings or something, or doing their nails, getting ready for the week's work. Anyway, you can see it linked up. There's all the statements and so on in there, and I wish you luck. He does tie up to your victim?"

"Oh, definitely, I'd say." Mendoza gave him a brief run-down on Cindy Hamilton. "You didn't turn anything at all?"

"Not a thing," said Barth. "We went the usual route. All of 'em said they'd very definitely recognize him, but none of them picked out any mug shots. We wasted a hell of a lot of time dusting all those places for latents and weeding out prints of all their friends who might have left any around, and didn't get one damn thing. He wasn't wearing gloves, so he's just careful—or lucky. NCIC didn't have a thing on the M.O. or the description, and he didn't show in our records where we looked first. So now you can go look in all the same places and come up empty."

"Hell," said Hackett unemphatically. "What a bastard to work. He damn near killed this one too. She only came to this morning—concussion and about twenty knife wounds. It looked as if he'd knocked her against the stereo cabinet. She put up quite a fight, by the look of the place."

"Yeah." Barth nodded. "So did all of ours—and the Spencer girl—but he's big and tough, and he doesn't care how much damage he does. Do have fun chasing him, boys." He got up. "I'm going home. Thank God it's my day off tomorrow. Let me know if you catch up with him, but I won't hold my breath."

As he went out, Mendoza eyed the fat folder idly, making no move to pick it up. "Inventive character," he said. "And a waste of time to speculate what the head doctors would say about him. I think I'll go home too, Arturo. We haven't had a lab report on the Hamilton girl's apartment. I suppose this time he could have left some prints, but if they're not in anybody's records—"

"How do we know?" asked Hackett. "The nothing they got from NCIC doesn't say a damned thing." It didn't, of course, because the National Crime Information Center's computers only numbered current crimes unsolved; when a case was cleared it was removed from the computers' memory. "Or have you got a hunch he's first time out?"

"No hunch—it could be, it doesn't have to be. The only thing I will say is that if we don't land on him, sooner or later he'll end up killing another girl. I wonder," said Mendoza, "why he's switched beats."

"We don't know that he has," said Hackett dampeningly. "He may just have spotted the Hamilton girl somewhere and it was chance she lives where she does."

"¿Como?" Mendoza pulled the folder onto the desk blotter and opened it, began to leaf through the reports. Five minutes later he said, "I don't think so, Art. Look at what a tight little circle it is—extraño—Fountain Avenue, Berendo, Kenmore, Harvard, Delongpre—and the homicide on Fountain again. All the addresses above Santa Monica, in old Hollywood—between Vermont and Western." After twenty-six years on this force, Mendoza knew his city by heart. "And now all of a sudden he's come all the way down here."

"If you feel like deducing from A to B," said Hackett, "I'll point out that an area like that—old uptown Hollywood —is the kind of place a lot of young women might live who're working for fairly small salaries. Cheaper rents, more convenient to public transportation if they don't drive. You aren't suggesting he picks victims by their addresses, are you?"

"I don't know, damn it. I just say it's a little odd." Mendoza shut the folder, leaned back and shut his eyes. "Wait for the lab report. Somebody had better type up a statement for the Hamilton girl to sign."

"Meaning me," said Hackett. "But right now I'm going home."

Mendoza picked up his hat and followed him out. In the corridor Higgins was talking to Sergeant Lake at the switchboard. He said to Mendoza, "Well, Willy finally came apart and gave us a statement. Just one more of the younger generation who doesn't believe in free-enterprise capitalism."

"Oh?" said Hackett. "Which way?"

"The supplier expected to get paid for the H—he was interested in profits all right. Willy was mad because he wouldn't extend credit."

"Go home," said Mendoza. "You're not supposed to be here at all."

"I know, I know." Thursday was normally Higgins' day off. "But the damn painters are at the house, and one of them keeps a transistor radio going. I hope to God they'll be finished tomorrow." He stretched and resettled his tie, which was under one ear as usual. "John took Willy down to book him." He drifted out.

In the communal office, their policewoman Wanda Larsen was arguing about something with a sleepy-looking Henry Glasser. There hadn't been any sign of Jason Grace since late this morning; he was probably out hunting possible heisters; but Galeano had come back from somewhere and was just sitting at his desk staring into space. Hackett went over and prodded him.

"Hey, *paisano*, it's end of shift." Galeano jumped and looked up. Hackett grinned at him. "Bridegroom daydreaming. Only three more days, Nick."

Galeano laughed. "As a mattter of fact," he said, "I was wondering if we're so smart to go to Yosemite for a honeymoon, after those couple of earthquakes up there last month."

"I've always said marriage is dangerous," said Glasser deadpan. Wanda made a grimace at him and got up, rummaging in her bag for keys.

By the time Higgins got home to the big old house in Eagle Rock, the painters had mercifully left for the day; they only had the back wall to finish and should complete the job tomorrow. Mary said she'd spent most of the day at the public library or she'd have gone mad. The house was quiet enough now, with Laura Dwyer busy over homework and Steve, expectably, in the new darkroom built onto the garage a couple of months ago. The little Scotty Brucie bounced underfoot.

Strangely enough, these days Higgins felt a little like a bridegroom himself, even if he and Mary had been married over three years. It wasn't that he had felt like an interloper in the house on Silver Lake Boulevard, but it was the house that Bert Dwyer had bought sixteen years back when he and Mary were expecting their first baby, and there were memories of Bert in it—Bert who had died on the marble floor of the bank with the heister's slugs in him.

These days, the Higginses were even more a solid family. It just slid vaguely through Higgins' mind as he bent to pick up their own baby, solid little Margaret Emily who was unbelievably two years old now, and just as pretty and smart as her mother.

Hackett was getting used to the longer drive these four months since they'd moved to the new house high in Altadena; on the freeway it didn't take that much longer, unless there was a jam. But they weren't on daylight saving yet, and it was dark when he got home.

He kissed Angel; the children were for once playing quietly, Mark with a coloring book and Sheila with her beloved stuffed cats. It was good to be home, after a boring day. He sat down to look at the *Herald* before dinner, and he wasn't thinking at all about the offbeat rapist or the other things they were working on.

As Mendoza approached the tall iron gates, high on the hill above Burbank—the wrought-iron gates leading to Alison's new country estate—he squinted up at them in the last rays of the dying sun and reflected that his red-haired Scots-Irish girl had been right again. These days she had one resigned phrase for any new problems arising: it all went to show, she said, how one thing led to another.

Certainly her love affair with the ancient Spanish hacienda had led her to spend a lot of money on updating it; and the chain-link fence enclosing four and a half acres had only been the beginning. There had been the construction of an apartment in what had been the old winery for Ken and Kate Kearney, the latest additions to the household. Kearney, a retired rancher, would of course know all about the ponies for the twins, she had said, and so of course he did; and plump little Kate Kearney would be such a help to Mairí in the house.

The ponies had materialized; that had meant creating a stable out of one of the outbuildings. The ponies, a Welsh pair of dark bays named Star and Diamond for their white face markings, were a great success with the twins, but they had further necessitated the construction of a riding ring and corral alongside the stable. And it was too dark to spot them now, but somewhere on the hill would be the Five Graces, the sheep recommended by Kearney to keep the wild undergrowth eaten down.

Mendoza climbed out of the Ferrari, opened the gates, drove through and got out to close them. The gates bore the name of the house in intricate letters at the top: *La Casa de la Gente Feliz*, the house of happy people.

There were some California live oaks on the four and a half acres, but Alison had said leave most of it wild, just some landscaping around the house. In the last couple of months she had been spending quite a lot more money, and the landscaping had gone in—fairly mature Italian cypress trees, hibiscus bushes against the house, modest sweeps of lawn at front and sides, a few avocado and orange trees on either side of the curving driveway, more hibiscus flanking the triple garage. At the moment she had decided that the Kearneys' car deserved a garage too, and that was half built as an addition to the apartment, with a hundred yards of new drive to be added later.

And what was passing through Mendoza's mind now was—one thing leading to another—that it was damned inconvenient to have to stop and open and shut those gates, going and coming. There would probably be some way to install an automatic opener, something on the principle of those garage-door openers, he thought.

In fact, only one of the potential problems attendant on the move had astonishingly resolved itself. Everybody had been nervous about the juxtaposition of the redoubtable half-Siamese El Señor and the Kearneys' large black cat Nicodemus. But it appeared that territorial rights established a truce. The

Kearneys had moved into their apartment a month before the Mendozas and Mairí MacTaggart had moved into the house; and by the time the four Mendoza cats had gone out exploring their new domain, Nicodemus had occupied by right the entire area around the old winery, the stable, corral and riding ring, and the grove of live oaks on that side of the hill. After a few bristly encounters with a good deal of hissing and spitting, El Señor—who only pretended to be a great warrior in any case—had tacitly reserved for his own domain the other half of the property, and a peaceable truce was in effect.

The other potential problem had been solved by the discovery of an excellent parochial school only a mile away down the hill. It even boasted a small kindergarten; but time sliding by as alarmingly as it did, next September the twins, Johnny and Teresa, would be starting first grade.

However, that gate . . . It was nearly full dark when he slid the Ferrari into the garage beside Alison's Facel-Vega and pulled down the door. There were lights in the house, welcoming. As if to add further welcome, from somewhere out there in the dark a couple of the Five Graces uttered loud bass *baas*.

Halfway up the new cement path from garage to back door, he was pounced on playfully by the Old English sheepdog Cedric, and being taken unawares and off balance, fell flat on his face. "*¡Vaya por Díos!* Down—*bastante!* No, I don't want to play—down, damn it!" Fuming, he marched in the back door.

Alison and Mairí were both in the big kitchen beyond the generous service-porch-pantry, Alison making a salad at the sink and pink-cheeked silver-haired Mairí peering into the oven. "Now I will tell you," began Mendoza, "that damned dog—"

"Oh, you're home, darling, I didn't hear the car." The twins, however, had, and came running.

"Daddy, Daddy, we been ridin' all afternoon—an' Uncle Ken let us *gallop* a lot—Johnny was almost afraid—"

"I wasn't neither, an' Diamond galloped faster than Star—Uncle Ken says I'm better 'n Terry because my legs are longer —but, Daddy—"

"Yes, yes, *niños*. You're both very good indeed. I will tell you, *querida*," said Mendoza, "we've got to put a light on that path from the garage. This damned dog you saddled us with —I might have broken my neck. And another thing—" Sheba landed on his shoulder from behind without warning. "Cats!" he said. "Dogs! And I'll tell you something else—"

"Now calm down, *chico*," said Alison.

"The man needs a dram or two before dinner," said Mairí.

"We galloped *lots* and Star can gallop just as fast as Diamond, an' I only had to hang on a little bit—"

"Uncle Ken says we both gonna be good riders—only it'd be more fun outside the fence. Daddy, can't we ride outside the fence?"

As if by magic, hearing a reference to strong drink, El Señor arrived, floated up to the counter under the cupboard where the liquor was kept, and uttered a raucous demand.

"*¡Santa Maria!* How did I ever get into all this?" demanded Mendoza violently.

"Now, now," said Mairí. "Take the man away and settle him down before dinner, *achara*. It will be half an hour and a bit. He's doubtless had a bothersome day. I'll see to the salad."

Alison poured El Señor his half ounce of rye, put a shot glass, the bottle of rye and a glass of sherry on a tray and shepherded Mendoza down to the huge square living room, Cedric bouncily preceding them and the twins in hot pursuit. The other two cats, Bast and Nefertite, were sound asleep on the oversize couch at right angles to the fieldstone hearth. The new one was slumbering peacefully on a blanket in the middle of the floor; the new one, Luisa Mary, not so new now at nearly eight months old, was astonishingly mobile when awake and by now had a full head of hair as outrageously red as Alison's. She was also definitely, as Mairí had predicted, going to be left-handed.

"Now sit down and relax," said Alison.

He swallowed rye and began to feel slightly better. "A post or something with a floodlight," he said. "Or a floodlight on that side of the garage. And another thought I had—that gate —it is one big damned nuisance, having to open and shut it. If there was an electric eye or something—"

"Yes, I know," said Alison, sipping sherry. "I'd had the same thought, but we've spent so much money already—"

"Damn it, might as well be hanged for a sheep as a lamb," said Mendoza.

"Yes. Well—that's another thing," said Alison. "Those sheep. They ought to be sheared, Ken says. They were a year old in February, and sheep ought to be sheared once a year."

"I suppose he can locate somebody to do it."

"I hope so. About the gate, I'll look in the yellow pages and get an estimate on the electric eye. You know, Luis, it is very funny, isn't it, how one thing keeps leading to another."

"Daddy, you didn't listen about the *galloping*—"

"And about ridin' outside the fence. Please, Daddy—"

The new one woke up and began to bellow. Alison swooped to pick her up.

Mendoza resignedly poured himself another shot of rye.

Friday was Nick Galeano's day off, but he wouldn't be getting together with his bride-to-be; according to what they'd heard she was a very proper convent-bred girl, and quite thick with Galeano's mother. It was likely all the women—he had several sisters—were busy over clothes and protocol for the wedding.

The night watch had, expectably, left them a couple of new ones. A lab report had gotten sent up after everybody left last night, and Mendoza looked at that before reading Piggott's report.

"Well, there you are," he said to Hackett, passing it over. It was the lab report on Cindy Hamilton's apartment. "A great big blank. Latents picked up—not many—all belong to her or these couple of close girl friends—the one who found her, another one. She doesn't have a steady boy friend. The one girl said she'd had a spat with the fellow she'd been going with, and it hadn't been serious anyway. You went out on him before we heard what she had to say, and turned up an alibi—at that party for his mother's birthday, and that's irrelevant now. Now we know it was Dapper Dan."

"And where the hell to go on it—"

"Well, there isn't anywhere," said Mendoza irritably. "Unless—¡por Dio! That's woolgathering."

"What?"

"He told them all he'd just landed here from back East—no particular place specified. Could that be so, Art? Just maybe? Maybe somewhere back East a Dapper Dan was operating, and the lawmen there gave up on him, and the M.O. got erased out of NCIC's computers."

"You do have useful ideas," said Hackett. "So we send queries to every force east of the Mississippi asking?"

Mendoza didn't bother to answer that obvious question; he picked up the night report as Hackett went out to the communal office. They were now working five heist jobs, and on two of them had good descriptions: a pair, by the descriptions, had pulled both jobs last week, and were fairly distinctive—a Mutt-and-Jeff pair, both black, one big, one little, and they sounded like a pair of bunglers. On the first job they had dropped half the loot in getting away, and one witness had passed on a description of the car, an old clunker of a Ford, dirty white. Palliser and Grace were working that; Landers, Glasser and Wanda went out on the others. There was still a statement to get from the second liquor-store clerk on Monday night's heist, and Hackett was waiting for him to show as promised when Mendoza erupted from his office with the night report in his hand.

"For God's sake, of all the ridiculous things—the jungle getting hairier all the time, and there's got to be a first for everything, but for *God's* sake . . . Jimmy, you'd better contact these people and ask them to come in to make a statement as soon as possible. I want to hear about this one firsthand."

"What's up?" asked Higgins, looking up from his typewriter. "Dogs!" said Mendoza.

They came in about ten o'clock, a good-looking couple, Mr. and Mrs. Thomas Pryor. Pryor was a lawyer; they lived in West Hollywood. They were middle-aged, he lean and dark, she frosted blond and smartly dressed.

"Listen," said Pryor, "do you think I was about to take a chance? The crime rate up—a lot of people keep these attack-trained dogs now. Would you have chanced it? Well, I didn't."

His wife shivered. "It certainly looked terribly savage."

They had gone to the Dorothy Chandler Pavilion, to a concert, last night, and come out to the parking lot rather late— Mrs. Pryor had been kept waiting in the ladies' room. And as they approached their car, with the crowd thinned out and at the far end of the parking lot, they'd been accosted by a man with a dog.

"It was a great big Doberman," said Pryor, "and I know those damned things are dangerous. I couldn't give you any kind of description of the man, I'm sorry, he was about my size, maybe five ten, he had a hat pulled down over his face. He just said, this is a trained attack dog and I'll set him on you if you don't hand over your wallet."

"That's a first, all right," said Hackett, intrigued. "And you did?"

"It looked awfully ferocious," said Mrs. Pryor. "I was scared to death."

The man with the Doberman had gotten about seventy dollars from Pryor's wallet. But interestingly, he hadn't taken anything but the cash, ignoring the various pieces of jewelry they both were wearing. He'd just walked up the alley out of the lot, and that was that.

"It was just ravening to be ordered to attack," said Mrs. Pryor. "I've always been terrified of Dobermans anyway."

"And just where," said Mendoza to Hackett, "do we go on that one?"

31

TWO

There didn't seem to be much to do about the man with the
Doberman. As a gesture, Mendoza sent a query to R. and I.
about the *modus operandi*: did anybody have a record anywhere of such a caper? It was a new and novel M.O. to the
Central beat, but didn't offer any leads.

Landers and Glasser brought in a possible suspect on one
of the heists; Mendoza sat in on the questioning, but it was
inconclusive, up in the air. They let him go while Landers
went to check the offered alibi.

Mendoza and Hackett presently went out to lunch together,
at Federico's up on North Broadway, and coming back to the
office at one-fifteen met Palliser just coming in with a witness;
he introduced them. "Mr. Henry Simms. Mr. Simms," said
Palliser, "has a funny little story to tell us."

"Well, I guess you can call it funny," said Simms. "And I
don't know that I believe it myself." He was a stout, short,
pugnacious-jawed fellow about sixty-five, in neat and clean
sport shirt and slacks. He took the chair Palliser pulled out for
him and regarded them dubiously. "This is the damnedest

thing I ever ran across. Joe! Of all people, Joe getting killed like that."

"Mr. Simms was a friend of Mr. Kelly's," said Palliser.

"Well, I was," said Simms as if there'd been some argument about it. "You see, while Joe was working he'd gotten transferred around so much by the railroad, him and his missus hadn't ever bought a house. Just rented. Myra and me had—I was in carpentry and cabinetmaking all my life—we had a nice little place over in Lincoln Heights, but the goddamn state took it, when they were expandin' the Golden State freeway they just took it, some damn thing called eminent domain —give me twenty-five thousand, I coulda sold it for forty then if I'd wanted to, which I didn't. Damn government. And it was along about then Myra died, so that's how come I'm in the apartment on Miramar and got to know Joe. We ran into each other at the market, and got talking. We had the same kind o' background, thought the same way about things, 'round about the same age and all—both of us widowers without much to do, y'know? We used to get together, him living only a block away—I got a color TV, and we'd play checkers sometimes. I don't know how much there is to this, though I'm bound to say Joe wasn't a fellow to go imagining things." He cocked his head at them.

"For what it's worth—" said Palliser.

"Well. I couldn't believe it, about Joe. Mr. Moreno, fellow lives across from him and found him, he knew Joe and I were friends, he called me after he called the cops. I was just, well, flabbergasted. Joe! Who'd want to knife Joe, for Gossakes? There's no sense to it at all. He wasn't even robbed—nine bucks and some change on him, you said, didn't you? It just don't make no sense. But I just got to thinking about what he said on Wednesday, and that don't make no sense either but, I mean, there it *is*. Which sounds sort of silly, but now this has happened, well, Joe wasn't no fool."

"He told you about this on Wednesday," prompted Palliser.

" 'S right. Wednesday afternoon on his way home. He said he thought this guy was following him, see. He noticed him

33

first at the library—Joe was a great one for Westerns, he went to the library about once a week regular—and then he spotted him at the market, and then, he said, be damned if the guy wasn't on the bus when he started home. And seemed to be watching him sort of funny. I thought he must be imagining things, though that wasn't like Joe. It was probably just a coincidence, but—well, it's funny."

"Did he tell you what the fellow looked like?" asked Hackett.

"He just said, a young fellow—blond, ordinary clothes, ordinary sort of looks, nobody he ever recalled seeing before. It sounds crazy—Joe just an ordinary guy, never did any harm to anybody, nobody have any reason to—but now this happens, it sort of sticks in my mind, y'know? But it is crazy. Somebody knifing Joe. Mr. Moreno said he never heard a thing, after he heard Joe leave about an hour before—and he would have, if Joe had had time to yell or put up a fight—just there he was, all bloody and the bag of groceries scattered around—" He shook his head. "Crazy. Sergeant Palliser seems to think—"

"Well, it's interesting," said Palliser.

"So somebody had time to rob him," said Mendoza.

"Yes, that's the point," said Palliser absently. "A little offbeat."

"Well," said Hackett, "it may mean something or not, but I can't see any connection with your Skid Row derelict."

Palliser rubbed his jaw thoughtfully. "I never said there was, Art. Except, funnily enough, there was a kind of resemblance—they were both in the sixties, middle-sized, sandy coloring—that's just coincidence. Hell, he could have imagined this, but why should he?"

"But why in hell should anybody be shadowing Joe?" asked Simms reasonably.

Palliser said, "Well, I'll get a statement typed up for you to sign. God knows what it means, but we'll put it in the record."

"Whatever you say. Just, after it happened, I got to thinking about it, y'know." Simms sat back and looked interestedly about the big office.

Higgins came in with another suspect heister to question, and Hackett went to sit in on that, which was also inconclusive. The suspect offered an alibi; he'd been at a big party and a lot of people would say so. What that was worth was moot; he had quite a long record, was four months on parole from a charge of attempted homicide, and his associates were probably of the same ilk. But they had to go through the motions. Hackett went out to start checking while Higgins wrote the follow-up report.

Mendoza wandered down the hall to the coffee machine about two forty-five; Grace and Landers were just coming in with another possible suspect. "Nick and Henry are killing time down in R. and I. waiting for those witnesses to pore over the mug shots," said Grace. "I think myself Mutt and Jeff are newcomers to the crime scene—pair of morons, they'd have been dropped on before now, and nobody's made them yet, and the lab did pick up some latents from the register on that first job." His regular-featured chocolate-brown face with its narrow mustache as neat as Mendoza's registered amused annoyance. "It's a dull job lately—nothing but these damn stupid heisters. To think anybody can still imagine it's a glamorous exciting job—and when I think of all the offbeat complex mysteries in the damn-fool detective novels—"

"Don't complain, or we may come in for a couple of those," said Mendoza sardonically. He took his cup of coffee back to his desk and sat looking out over the city view, ruminating idly on Mr. Simms, and desultorily on the man with the Doberman. There was no going anywhere on that, of course.

When the new call went down at three-thirty, everybody else was out or interrogating suspects, and Mendoza went out on it with Higgins.

It was an old apartment building, about sixteen units, on Vendome down from Beverly. The black-and-white squad was sitting in front; mostly on the Central beat they ran two-man cars, and Patrolman Zimmerman was at the entrance waiting for them, said Gomez was upstairs securing the scene. "Looks like some sort of O.D.," he told them. "Maybe suicide. Hell of a thing, the little kid found her. The daughter, kid about ten or eleven. She went to the neighbor, who called us. Mrs. Werner, it's apartment fourteen—the corpse is next door in sixteen. A Mrs. Marion Cooper."

It was a shabby old building, the rents probably middling low. Up the uncarpeted stair and down a narrow dark hall they came to Patrolman Gomez, massive in navy uniform, being noncommittally polite to a plump middle-aged woman.

"I don't understand what you mean by an O.D.—why, she was just a young woman, I know young people can have heart attacks too but—heavens, it's just terrible to think of Harriet finding her like that. What could have happened? . . ." She'd had a shock, and the talk was compulsive, but she looked like a normally sensible woman, plainly dressed, graying dark hair.

"Mrs. Werner," said Gomez, looking relieved at the advent of Mendoza and Higgins. "These are the detectives, ma'am."

"We'll want to talk to you shortly," Higgins told her.

"All right. I've got— I brought Harriet into my place. It seemed— She's only eleven. I suppose we ought to call her father. I just don't understand—I didn't know Mrs. Cooper very well, but she was just a young woman, couldn't be much over thirty—"

"We'll get back to you," said Higgins. She retreated into her own apartment, and Gomez edged the door of apartment sixteen farther open with one toe.

"It looks like an O.D. There doesn't seem to be any suicide note."

Mendoza stopped inside the threshold and looked around with distaste. Expectably, in an apartment of this vintage, the walls needed painting, the furniture was old and dun-colored; but the little living room hadn't been cleaned or straightened for some time, there were clothes and dirty dishes on every surface in wild disarray, and the place smelled stale and fusty. Past the living room to the left was a glimpse of a small kitchen with just enough space for a tiny square table and a couple of chairs at one end. In the other direction a minute cross hall led directly to a small square bathroom, a pair of equally small bedrooms to each side.

The body was in the bedroom on the left, quite peacefully reposing in the bed. "The covers were all pulled up," said Gomez apologetically. "We had to see if she might still be breathing, but—"

She looked to be about thirty, and no dead body is beautiful but they could see that she'd been a pretty woman: a taffy blonde, with a heart-shaped face, a small pouting mouth, and in the low-cut blue nylon nightgown her figure was curvaceous. She had died easily and comfortably without struggle. One hand was curled up around her head, a small plump hand with the nails painted dark red. The bedroom was in disorder too, the top of the bureau and dressing table heaped with miscellany, clothes on the one straight chair, the foot of the double bed; the door to the little closet was open, and that looked cluttered and untidy.

There was a little two-drawer nightstand at one side of the bed; it held a small ceramic lamp with a ruffled shade, an ashtray, and a used glass with a few dregs at the bottom. Higgins bent over and took a sniff. "Scotch."

"And maybe something else," said Mendoza. He looked at Gomez. "Get on the mike and rustle up a lab unit, will you?" He went out of the bedroom, across the living room, to the kitchen.

The sink was stacked with dirty dishes, but the little table was oddly clean and empty. Standing at one edge of the counter nearest the table was a pint bottle of a low-priced brand of scotch; there was only about a jiggerful left in it. "So," said Mendoza.

"Turn the lab loose on it. They'll give us all we'll get on this."

"Maybe," said Mendoza. When they came out to the hall, Gomez was coming back. He said a mobile unit was on the way.

The door of the next apartment was ajar. Mendoza tapped on it and went in. Mrs. Werner got up anxiously from a sagging couch across the room. "Oh, have you found out anything? What have you—"

"Are you the policemen?" asked a thin little voice.

"Yes, that's right," said Mendoza.

"What—what happened to Mama?" She was a nice-looking little girl, if not exactly pretty: thin and pale, with dark-brown hair in a modified Dutch bob, and steady hazel-green eyes, a straight little mouth.

"Our doctor will find out," said Mendoza. He hesitated; questioning a child could be tricky; but she looked back at him gravely and began to answer questions unasked.

"She never got up as early as me, I always get my own breakfast. Her alarm's set for eight, so she can get the nine-fifteen bus—she doesn't have to go to work till ten, see. So I—I never saw her this morning—it wasn't till I got home from school—I saw she was still—still in bed, and it was funny—" Suddenly the square little chin quivered, and she clamped her jaw tight. "I thought—I'd better ask somebody—if she was sick—"

"You did just right, honey," said Mrs. Werner.

Mendoza sat down uninvited. "What about last night, Harriet?" he asked gently. "Did your mother have a friend come, or was she out somewhere? Or—"

"Oh, she was out. Like usual," said Harriet. She sounded surprised that he hadn't known that. "She went out most nights, someplace where there were people to talk to, and TV. Barney's, or the Ace-High Bar, mostly. I was asleep when she came home, I usually am. I didn't hear her come home, but this morning I saw—I saw she was in bed—just like usual, and—" She swallowed. "Please," she said, "she's—she's dead, isn't she?"

Nobody said anything until Mrs. Werner got out stiffly, "Yes, honey, I'm afraid she is."

"I thought—prob'ly she was," said Harriet. A tear rolled down one cheek, and she sniffed valiantly. "I suppose—somebody'd better call Daddy. I mean Grandma. Daddy'll be at work, but Grandma's usually home."

Mrs. Werner, who had sat down again, got up with sudden decision and said to Harriet, "Yes, we'll do that in just a minute. I just want to talk to the officers a little while, you stay here, honey." She led them out to the hall, and shut the door behind them, went down the hall. She had a rather sheeplike face, and continually reached to push overlarge fashionable spectacles up on her nose, but her eyes were unexpectedly intelligent. "Now I don't know anything about this," she told them uncompromisingly, "but I guess neither do you yet, and I might as well tell you what I do know about Mrs. Cooper."

"Yes, Mrs. Werner?" Mendoza waited interestedly.

"Which isn't all that much, but a woman can read another woman, you take me. That's a nice little girl in there, nicer than you'd expect a woman like that to have. But I don't think there was any harm in her—she was just flighty. Sort of, you know, irresponsible. She held a job—she was a waitress at a coffee shop on Beverly," and she named it. "I've only been in her place a time or two, we didn't neighbor, but you could see she was a terrible housekeeper—dressed herself up like a bandbox, but that was as far as it went. And she left Harriet alone a lot too much, even when she first moved here four years ago when Harriet was just a little thing. She was divorced from Harriet's father, he has her on weekends, I only met him once but he seems like a real nice steady fellow."

"I see," said Mendoza.

"She didn't die of anything natural, did she?" she asked shrewdly. "Well, all I'll say is, I don't think there was any harm in her. She didn't throw wild parties, or bring men home, or get drunk or anything. I was sorry for the little girl, she wasn't any kind of mother to her, but that's the worst anybody could say."

"Thanks very much," said Mendoza.

"I suppose somebody had better phone the father. I mean, she can't be left alone, and he always has her weekends—"

Mendoza and Higgins consulted mutely and shrugged at each other. That certainly made more sense than taking the child to Juvenile Hall. They went back to the Cooper apartment and found Duke and Scarne just finishing the photography. There was an address book beside the phone in the living room, and Duke told them to keep their paws off it, nothing had been printed yet. "Preserve calm," said Mendoza, and used his pen to turn the pages. There was a number for *Dan* listed under the C's. "Disorganized females." He went back to the apartment next door.

"Yes, sir, that's right, Dan's my daddy. It's El Centro Street in South Pasadena."

Back in the Ferrari, Mendoza lit a cigarette and used the phone on the dashboard while Higgins made some notes for a first report. He got a sensible-sounding female who took the news calmly with only a few exclamations and questions. She said her son drove a city bus, on a Hollywood route; he wasn't due home until seven o'clock, and she didn't have a car available. If the neighbor could kindly keep Harriet until then, her father would be right over to pick her up. Would that be all right? Mendoza reassured her, resignedly climbed stairs again to pass that on to Mrs. Werner.

It was a quarter past five. There would be places to ask questions on this, but they probably couldn't ask intelligent ones until they'd heard what the lab had to say. Higgins agreed with that and said he'd half promised to take the family out to dinner and it would be nice to get home early. "The city pays you to put in eight hours," said Mendoza, and swung the Ferrari onto Beverly Boulevard.

The coffee shop where Marion Cooper had been a waitress was one of a chain, a bright and scrupulously clean big place.

Just inside the front door was a cashier's counter; the girl perched on the stool behind it was about thirty, synthetically attractive with a little too much makeup, slightly protruding teeth. She stared at the badge. "The m-manager?" she said. "Mr. Boatman? He's in the back—what's it about?"

Higgins said they were sorry to tell her that Mrs. Marion Cooper was dead. "We understand she worked here."

"Marion? Dead? Oh, my God!" she said. "Oh, my God— how? How could she be dead? She's only thirty-one—"

"We're not sure yet," said Mendoza, "but it looks as if it could have been suicide."

She drew her head back stiffly, and her expression was utterly blank for ten seconds, and then she said, "Marion? She'd be the last person in the world—I'll never believe that! She's always right on top, I never knew her to worry about anything—that just couldn't *be*—I can't believe she— Oh, Mr. Boatman!" She tumbled down off the stool and ran around the counter toward the man just emerged from the door marked *Private* at the back of the restaurant. "Mr. Boatman, it's police—and they say—"

He was a big egg-shaped man with shrewd dark eyes and the remnants of a Brooklyn accent. He ushered them out smoothly to the foyer, away from the customers inside, and listened to what they had to say with obvious astonishment.

"Now I don't know what facts you got hold of," he said, "and I don't know what you want from me, gentlemen. I just knew the girl as an employee. But one thing I'll tell you right off the bat. That one a suicide? Like Sam Goldwyn put it, in two words, impossible. That little nitwit didn't have the brains to get depressed enough."

"Which," said Higgins back in the car, "is also interesting. And it's five past six. If you don't want to go home, I do, and seeing I missed my day off this week I think I'll stay home tomorrow."

When Mendoza got home, Alison informed him that she'd found the people to install the electric eye, but they'd also have to take all the cars in to a garage to have a gadget installed to make the electric eye work. And it would take about a full day, but it couldn't be helped.

"Oh, hell," said Mendoza. But it would be worth it, for the convenience.

"And they can't come until next week. But when we know it'll get done eventually . . . I never realized how awkward it was going to be, having to open and shut those gates—"

"Just," said Mendoza, "one thing leading to another again, my love."

Landers was off on Saturday, and with the wedding this near, Galeano wasn't much use as a detective. There had been another heist at a pharmacy overnight; the clerk would be coming in to make a statement, look at the mug shots.

Before he did, the cashier from the chain coffee shop, whose name was Marge Colbert, and one of the waitresses, Rena Hiller, showed up as arranged to answer some questions. They had both known Marion Cooper well. She had worked at the coffee shop for four years or so. "Ever since she got the divorce," said Marge Colbert. "Maybe she wasn't the brainiest girl around—I heard what old Boatman said to you yesterday—but she was always nice, nice to be around, everybody liked Marion, she was always so cheerful and happy."

"All right, what about any boy friends?" asked Hackett.

The two girls exchanged glances. The Hiller girl was a defiantly bright blonde, a little buxom. "Well, yeah," she said. "We double-dated a few times. But it wasn't anything serious with Marion, she didn't want to get married again. She just liked a good time, good company."

"Some names, please," said Mendoza.

"Just one lately," said Rena Hiller. "Jerry Wall. He's a nice guy, we all know him, he's in for lunch nearly every day, he works at a garage up on Vermont. That's how Marion met him."

"Were they shacking up?" asked Hackett bluntly.

Both girls looked a little shocked. "No, of course not," said

Marge Colbert. "You cops. Talk about the way your minds work. No, Marion wasn't that kind—honestly—and besides, she didn't want to lose the support money. Her husband had tried to get the kid, see, and if he could show she wasn't living straight, maybe he could get custody even now, and she knew that."

"We've heard," said Mendoza, "that she was out most evenings, at some place called Barney's, a bar somewhere. And you're telling us she was playing it all straight and virtuous? Had she been hitting the bottle at all?"

"Cops!" said Rena. "Listen, I know about that, but it wasn't the way you think. Marion—she just couldn't stand to be alone, you see? She liked people around, and talk. She didn't have a TV at home, and of course the kid is old enough so Marion could leave her—"

"Alone," said Hackett. "She's eleven, isn't she?"

"I guess so, around there. Marion knew one of the girls at that Ace-High place—one of the waitresses. And she could walk up there, and to the other place—she didn't have a car, she never could pass the driver's test. She'd just go up there for the evening to watch TV, talk to people. And no, she didn't drink much. She'd gotten to know some of the regulars at both those places, they're not cheap bars, really sort of family places—it was just, what was she supposed to do alone at home most nights?"

"What about her husband? Had he been bothering her any way?"

They both shook their heads. "If you mean did he want her to come back to him, no," said Rena. "And as long as he came through with the alimony and support, that was the way she wanted it. It wasn't all that much—he just drives a bus for the city—she had to work besides, but it made a difference."

"All right. Had she been worried or disturbed about anything recently?"

"Marion?" said Marge. "I told you, she never was. Nothing ever got her down. She was just the same as always, last time we saw her on Thursday. When she didn't come in yesterday,

I tried to get her on the phone even before Mr. Boatman told me to, but no luck. We thought maybe she was sick—she hardly ever was, but just after Christmas she had an abscessed tooth and was off three days, I thought maybe—"

All that didn't give them much. They got down the statements, as preliminary information; they might or might not hear something from the lab today. And they'd want to talk to the ex-husband as well as the boy friend.

"And I suppose," said Mendoza meditatively, "we ought to talk to Harriet again. And ask around at those nice family places about anybody she might have picked up there."

"But, Luis—it's all the wrong shape," said Hackett. "If she'd been biffed on the head, something like that, it'd be easy to read—the good-time girl picking up with the wrong guy. But an O.D. of some kind?"

"I know, I know. Arguing ahead of data again. Wait to see what the autopsy says—and the lab."

"You haven't had any luck yet?" Palliser slid the car into the curb and stepped on the brake. They both got out.

"It is," said Jason Grace gloomily, "all these goddamned abortions. Aside from the fact that it's morally wrong, it's made it practically impossible to find a baby to adopt. It's not as if we're being fussy—it'd be nice to have a boy, but another girl would be just fine too." The Graces already had a much-loved little girl, Celia Anne, who'd be over two years old now. "We've had applications in all over for six months, damn it."

"That's tough," said Palliser.

"And you're just lucky you can produce your own," said Grace amiably.

Palliser laughed. "I wouldn't have agreed with you when he was still waking us up at two A.M. every night." But young David was long past that stage now, starting to walk. "I hope this fellow's home."

"What you tell me, it's a handful of nothing," said Grace. "If funny."

"Oh, yes," said Palliser. "That all right."

The apartment house on Miramar Street where Joe Kelly had lived was old but solid-looking, and fairly well kept up, with some sketchy landscaping in front and an old-fashioned front porch. In the little lobby was a block of twelve mailboxes along one wall, but Palliser didn't glance at it, made for the stairs. The place was very quiet. Upstairs, he led Grace down to the middle of the hall and stopped, reaching for the bell beside the door marked nine. "Right here?" said Grace.

"Yep." In the center of the worn carpet was an irregular dark stain, where Joe Kelly had fallen and died. The door opened. "Mr. Moreno?"

"That's me." He was a tall thin old man with a little fringe of gray hair around his ears. "What can I do for you?" He peered at Palliser. "Oh, it's the sergeant again. I don't know what more I could tell you, but come in."

"This is Detective Grace."

"How do. Set down. The wife's out, but I could get us some coffee—"

"Never mind, thanks. We heard something a little queer from Mr. Simms, and we just wondered whether Mr. Kelly had mentioned it to you. You knew him fairly well, I take it."

"That's so. You don't mean what Joe thought about some fellow following him around?" Moreno slid a veined old hand up his jaw. "That's foolish. Yes, he did mention it to me. Sure I knew Joe—lived across the hall four-five years. It is hell to get old, can't do much no more, and everything so damned expensive, can't afford to go any place—nice weather, I'd go down and sit on the front porch most afternoons, and Joe'd stop to chew the fat now and then. I saw him Wednesday afternoon when he come home, he told me about that. I thought he was imagining things—foolishness."

"What do you think about it now?" asked Palliser.

Moreno said soberly, "I don't know, Sergeant."

"What exactly did he say?" asked Grace.

"Said he noticed this fellow first at the public library, and then he was at the market at the same time, and got on the same bus. Well, nothing in that—a lot of people live around here and go the same places. But Joe said the fellow kept staring at him."

"And since Thursday, what do you think about it?" persisted Palliser.

"Well, I was shook up all right, about that happening to Joe," said Moreno slowly. "Never so flabbergasted in my life. We hadn't heard a thing—I heard his door slam about an hour before, when he left, but this place is pretty well built. The wife asked me to go see if the mail had come, we was expecting a letter from our daughter in Oakland—and then when I opened the door, there's Joe bleeding like a stuck pig." He shook his head. "Crime rate up, and this isn't the best part of town. Well—somebody following Joe? Somebody with a reason to kill him? Excuse me, Sergeant, but it still sounds like foolishness. Joe was a nice guy, but he wasn't anybody special. He didn't have anything anybody wanted—where was any reason to kill him?"

It was a reasonable question, considering that Kelly hadn't been robbed of the little he'd had on him.

Downstairs, Grace said, "He was imagining things. And some punk followed him in to grab his wallet, Kelly fought back and got stabbed, and the punk lost his nerve and ran."

"Off the top of your mind, Jase. The punk followed him all the way upstairs and Kelly didn't notice? The punk would have tackled him as soon as he got inside—and that's very unusual behavior for a punk, following somebody inside a building. The general rule is, the quick shove and grab for the wallet."

"True," said Grace. "You're right, John, the setup is very funny. How do you read it?"

"As far as I can see," said Palliser, "there's only one way it can have happened, which makes it all the funnier. Kelly came in with his bag of groceries and got upstairs, nearly to his own door, before X stabbed him. Which says that X was up there waiting—down at the end of the hall, it's fairly dark up there—and rushed him, probably as he was getting out his keys."

"But—" said Grace.

"I know. Kelly? Inoffensive little pensioner, no family, few friends, no money, no apparent vices. Or enemies."

"Well, whatever, there's just nothing to follow up. It's a dead end."

"Oh, you don't have to tell me that," said Palliser.

Mendoza was on the phone to the lab, after talking to Dr. Bainbridge's office about expediting the autopsy, and Hackett idly listening in, when a new call went down at three o'clock. Sergeant Farrell, sitting on the switchboard on Lake's day off, buzzed Glasser and said, "New homicide call. Barrett just called in. It's Cortez Street."

"No rest for the wicked." Glasser took down the address. Wanda was already on her feet; she was bucking for detective rank and ever eager for more street experience. Following her down to the elevator, Glasser rather sadly admired her sleek blond hair and trim figure in the navy uniform; a little waste, he thought, but try to argue with a determined female. In the parking lot she slid into the Gremlin beside him and found the County Guide on the dashboard shelf.

"It's down toward Temple, off Glendale Boulevard—"

"Such a helpful girl. I know where it is," said Glasser.

It was an old, old part of town. Everything had been there a long time, and hadn't seen much in the way of repair or remodeling. The black-and-white was sitting outside a ramshackle three-storey frame house once painted white. There was a sign in a front window, *Rooms by week or month.* On the narrow front porch, Patrolman Barrett was waiting for them with a woman. He looked at them with undisguised relief, a little warm admiration for Wanda in his eyes which annoyed Glasser. "This is Mrs. Hopkins." And welcome to her, said his tone.

She was a lean little black-haired, black-eyed woman, ageless, with a hard mouth and a rasping voice, and she was in a repressed fury. "Fifteen dollars they owed me, and now where's it coming from? Nowhere, that's where! I know the police and their ways—take every scrap that's there and nobody'll ever see it again, and I can whistle for my money—and all that bloody mess for somebody to clean up, adding insult to injury—"

"Let's look at what we've got, shall we?" said Glasser. "We can talk about it later."

She shut her teeth with an actual click. "Left end room on the top floor," she said acidly. "Cheapest I've got, five bucks a day. I saw the color of his money before I let 'em in, and he paid for two weeks and then quit. One suitcase between 'em, and I'd be surprised if they was really married."

"All right, all right, later," said Glasser. He and Wanda went in. The house had probably originally been a big family place with double parlors downstairs; now partitions had been put up to create many small rooms out of big ones. On the second floor, judging by the number of doors, the rooms were somewhat larger than closets; on the third, they looked like mere niches. The end door on the left was open, and they looked in.

The room might be seven by nine. It held a single iron bed, an ancient three-drawer chest, and a straight chair with one leg broken. There was a naked bulb hanging from the ceiling; the floor was stained bare pine, minus any carpet. Beside the bed was an open battered suitcase with a few clothes in it. At first glance there were a half dozen bottles scattered around, all empty except an upright fifth of vodka on the chest, a quarter full. Two dime-store tumblers lay on their sides in front of the suitcase.

The bodies were half on the bed, half on the floor. The girl had slid into a surprisingly graceful position, propped against the bed with her head thrown back; she had been a beautiful girl, with magnolia skin, long lustrous black hair, a model's figure. She was wearing a long white nylon nightgown, and the ugly dark stain on the left breast looked like an excrescence. The man was stretched out across the bed, legs sprawled down beside the girl: a good-looking man even in death, with plentiful curly gray hair, a square handsome face; he stared blindly up at the stained ceiling, and his right hand flung out on the dirty sheet was still clasped around the gun. He was fully dressed in slacks and sport shirt.

"Um," said Glasser, and stepped delicately closer. "Old S. and W. thirty-eight. Not much reason for any elaborate lab work—let's see what shows." He looked through the suitcase: nothing but female underclothes. He heard Wanda opening drawers.

"Nothing even put away," she said. "Henry—"

"What?"

"Nothing. Just, it's such a dreary place to die, isn't it?"

Glasser grunted. He gave a tentative heave to the man's body and it lifted slightly, supine and limp. They were both long cold. Rigor would develop in about twelve hours and pass off a little faster; he would have a guess they'd been dead about twenty-four hours.

There was a billfold in the hip pocket. He opened it, and Wanda came to look over his shoulder. There wasn't much in it. Two single-dollar bills. An out-of-date driver's license for Gerald Bussard, an address in Bakersfield. A Social Security card in the same name.

"Well, that's him all right," said Glasser with a glance at the corpse. "Five-eleven, a hundred and seventy, gray and blue, forty-six—that was six years back. See if there's any family in Bakersfield to pay for a funeral."

"And I wonder—why?" said Wanda. "How did they come to it—and here?"

"You want to delve into human nature and all the ramifications of it," said Glasser, "you turn into a lady novelist and exercise the imagination. All we deal in are facts."

They went downstairs and asked questions. Mrs. Hopkins couldn't tell them much they wanted to know. "Paid up until Wednesday, and I tackled him when he come back that night —didn't like the looks of 'em to start with. He said he had a job, short-order cook at a greasy spoon over on Temple—no, they didn't have a car, showed up out of the blue two weeks ago Wednesday—I don't take people in out of charity, you know, and we all got to live—said he'd pay me next day, but he never, I never laid eyes on 'em that day, and I was watching—them laying low— And he musta done it yesterday afternoon when I was up there askin' about him—everybody else in the house at work, so nobody heard the shots—and they told me he got fired for bein' drunk on the job—stick me with all this mess, and I'll never see that fifteen dollars—"

"I'll toss you for who writes the report," said Glasser in the car. The lab truck had just pulled up; the morgue wagon would be coming.

"I don't mind," said Wanda. She sounded subdued. "You know, I think you're wrong, Henry. It's us who deal in the human nature. Ramifications of."

There wasn't much point in it, since Barth had queried the computers on it so recently, but Mendoza had sent the routine request to R. and I. on Dapper Dan's M.O. Nobody expected anything to turn up on that.

The lab, of course, always took its own sweet time; give the devil his due, they were always busy. But when Mendoza finally talked to Scarne about five o'clock, he got a little information, if unofficial.

"Well, we're not quite as rushed as usual, Lieutenant. You'll get a report sometime. We haven't gotten around to measuring quantities yet, just done the analysis—but off the record I can make a guess on what the autopsy'll say on the Cooper woman."

"¿Qué?"

"Phenobarb—either all by itself or combined with booze. Both the glass and that bottle of scotch were laced pretty heavy. We'll get around to actual amounts for you, and the exact prescription."

"And thank you so much," said Mendoza. He passed that on to Hackett.

"So what does it say, Luis? The kid was there. She'd have heard if anybody had come back with the woman—if there'd been an argument, a fight. And if you're still thinking about the casual pickup, it's ridiculous to say anybody like that would—"

"What I'm thinking about," said Mendoza, brooding over his long hands steepled together, "is salaries."

"Come again."

"The salaries the city pays its bus drivers, *chico*. It can't be a very magnificent sum. The alimony and child support would cut into it. Maybe pretty deep."

"But there's not a thing to say—"

"Not yet," said Mendoza.

Saturday night in inner-city L.A. can get a little hairy, but most of the problem belongs to the patrolmen riding the squads: the brawls, traffic accidents, drunks, family fights.

The night watch at Robbery-Homicide came on to wait for the calls. Matt Piggott and Bob Schenke had been sitting on night watch for quite a while and were used to it, but Rich Conway was still griping about getting transferred. For one thing, Conway was a man who liked the girls, and they liked him, and it cut into his dating time. Schenke was a settled bachelor and Piggott the earnest fundamentalist was married, but night watch was discommoding Conway.

For once it started out as a quiet Saturday night, and then within five minutes, just before ten o'clock, they got three calls at once, to three separate heists.

The one Piggott took was routine, and it was the Mutt-and-Jeff comic team again; this time one of them had dropped his gun on the way out. It was a drugstore down on Third; they hadn't gotten much.

The one Schenke took was a bar on First, and there was a good description from a lot of witnesses: a big fat Negro with a big gun.

The one Conway went out on was probably going to be more important. It was an all-night pharmacy on Sixth Street, and there had been a clerk and a pharmacist on duty.

"I never saw him come in," said the pharmacist shakily.

His name was Clyde Burroughs. "All of a sudden he was there
—with the gun—he said to Ken, don't you make a move, back
against the wall—and he said to me, I want all your pills, man,
all the uppers and downers you got, and the cash from the
register—and Ken—he just stepped back against that shelf of
vitamins, the way the guy told him, he wouldn't have tried
anything—but he made a noise, and it was just like a damn
snake striking, the guy fired at him point-blank. Well, I don't
know exactly, you'll have to look at the tab from the register
—but Ken—we weren't putting up any fight—"

Ken Price, the clerk, had taken a bullet in the lung and by
now would be in Intensive Care at Cedars–Sinai. It might turn
into a homicide.

"And he had a southern accent," said Burroughs. "Some
kind of southern accent. He said you-all."

THREE

The Landerses both had Saturday off, which was convenient, but sometimes it created hell on Sunday mornings. When the alarm went off, they both erupted out of bed half awake and rushed around in the usual frenzy. Phillippa Rosemary—whose parents had naturally not known when they christened her so fancily that she'd grow up to be a staid policewoman—said crossly, rummaging for clean stockings, "It starts to look more attractive all the time, staying home and starting a family. Nothing but a glorified office job, showing the mug shots to the citizens—at least you get out on the street." She had been down in Records and Information since graduating from the academy.

"That's what I've been telling you," said Landers. They left separately, and at that Landers was the first man into the office. Mendoza was always late on Sunday if he came in, which he usually did just to see what was going on, though it was supposedly his day off. Landers was looking at the report the night watch had left when everybody else came drifting in, Hackett and Higgins, Grace, Glasser, Palliser. He passed it over to Higgins, who said, "Hell. A hair-trigger heister—all we need."

Hackett called the hospital; the clerk, Ken Price, was still alive but in Intensive Care. The pharmacist, Clyde Burroughs, was coming in to look at mug shots.

"And that Hamilton girl was supposed to come in to look at pictures when she's out of the hospital," said Higgins.

"Dapper Dan," said Hackett. "None of the other girls made him, but we can always hope." He called the hospital again; Cindy Hamilton was due to be discharged tomorrow. "And another couple of new heists to work. Mutt and Jeff again, well, we're pretty sure they're not in our records, nobody's made them either, but there are pretty good descriptions on these other two. Some lead may show."

Burroughs came in a few minutes later, and most of them trooped down to R. and I. with him. Landers introduced him to Phil, who settled him down in a cubicle with a couple of big books of mug shots. The relevant information they had was fed into the computers, and presently Palliser and Grace were handed half a dozen records which might belong to the big fat Negro heister: all men with likely backgrounds. There were only a couple of recent addresses, but you had to start from where you were. They went out on the hunt for those, and five minutes later Glasser and Higgins received four possibles on the other one, the hair-trigger heister, just by the description. There wasn't any mention of a southern accent but the records didn't include hometowns; it gave them places to look.

Mendoza came in about eleven, looked at the night report. Nobody had brought in any suspects yet. "I want to talk to Cooper," he said, depositing Piggott's report tidily in the desk tray.

"I figured, which was the reason I stayed in," said Hackett.

"Damnation, Wanda's day off. I suppose we ought to take a female along for form's sake, talking to the child—"

"Her father'll be there, and I take it the grandmother."

"Yes." Mendoza swiveled around in the desk chair, put out

his cigarette, and picked up the phone. After an interval he talked to the same calm-sounding woman he'd reached on Friday, and was assured that Cooper was home and available.

It was an old California bungalow on a narrow residential street in South Pasadena. The woman who let them in was also comfortable-looking, a round gray-haired woman in the late fifties, with steady dark eyes behind metal-framed glasses; she looked, in her plain cotton dress and unfashionable old-lady shoes, like a good cook and housekeeper, which she probably was.

The combination living-dining room was furnished with a jumble of old comfortable pieces of furniture blending together into homeness. Daniel Cooper had been sitting in a big armchair opposite a modest TV on a stand, reading the *Times*; he got up hastily to greet them.

"I wondered when you'd want to talk to me," he said. "Do you know yet what—what caused her death?"

"We haven't had an autopsy report, Mr. Cooper, but it looks rather definite that it was an overdose of phenobarbital."

"Oh, no." He shook his head. "That's—unbelievable. You mean—she meant to? No." There wasn't any sign of Harriet. Mrs. Cooper sat down quietly on the couch, watching and listening.

"Just what do you mean by that, Mr. Cooper?" asked Mendoza.

Cooper said mechanically, "Sit down, won't you. I'm sorry, but—" He was as nondescript and ordinary as the house, about thirty-five, medium height, a little round-shouldered, starting to lose his sandy hair; he looked like a solid stable citizen, not very imaginative. He sat down in the armchair again and looked at them, in the pair of chairs opposite. He said, "Marion? I'll never believe she committed suicide. She wasn't the type. She liked living too much—she was scared of death and dying, anything connected. She was always, well, cheerful and happy—outgoing do they say?—maybe that was the trouble. I suppose I should think about making some funeral arrangements, but I don't know—"

Hackett told him he'd be informed when the body would be released. "She didn't have any family?"

"No. No. Her mother and father were killed in an accident when she was only sixteen, there was an aunt she lived with after that, but she's dead now too. I'd be the only one to—"

"What do you mean, that was the trouble?" asked Mendoza.

"Well, the way she was," said Cooper. "Always wanting to go out, socialize, dances or movies, anywhere. She was— immature. She was only nineteen when we got married, I thought she'd grow out of it, but . . . She just couldn't take responsibility. She didn't like housework or cooking, she didn't —well, do much of it. She thought—when the baby was on the way—that'd be fun, but after Harriet was born she was always complaining how much work it made. But—well, the eight years we were married—it wasn't good, or very—very comfortable, you know—but she was—" He hunted for words, came out with, "So damned cheerful. Happy. Irresponsible. I'd—maybe criticize her a little, she'd snap back or cry and three minutes later forget it. She'd never in this world have killed herself."

"That's interesting," said Mendoza noncommittally. "Which of you wanted the divorce?"

"Marion." He blinked and looked down at his hands. "I sort of resisted the idea on account of Harriet, and then I thought I might get custody—you see, it wasn't the usual thing, a man alone, I could give her a nice solid home with Mother—Dad finished paying off the house before he died eight years ago—but, well, judges tend to be unrealistic, I guess."

"We understand she was getting both alimony and child support," said Hackett.

"Yeah, that's right. It was a little piece out of what I make, but there it was. And at least I had Harriet on weekends, she was agreeable to that."

"Did you ever suspect that she was—mmh, misbehaving with other men, drinking too much, using any kind of dope?"

He looked astonished. "Marion? For God's sake, no! Where'd you get that idea? She had the right to date other men if she wanted—but Marion isn't—wasn't—the kind to go in for—"

His mother spoke up quietly. "No, to be fair about it she was a perfectly good-hearted girl." But her eyes held hidden anger. "Just irresponsible and lazy. She wasn't a good mother to Harriet, but by the grace of God Harriet's a sensible child, and at least we've had her a couple of days a week, give her a better background in life. She's so much like Dan, just naturally neat and clean and orderly."

"I still can't understand—how she died."

"Did she have trouble sleeping lately, would you know? Been taking any medication?"

"I don't know. She never did—when we were together. She didn't even like to take aspirin, it upset her stomach," said Cooper. "I suppose," he added suddenly, "it could have been an accident of some sort—some mistake. She was damn careless about a lot of things, if she'd had something like that around she could have mixed it up with something else, not realized she was taking it."

"That's possible," agreed Mendoza. "Mr. Cooper, do you mind if we ask Harriet a few questions? We'll try not to upset her."

Cooper shrugged. His mother got up, said, "She's in her room," and went out.

Cooper said miserably, "I can't believe she meant— Oh, my God, if she'd been in any trouble of any kind she'd have known I'd try to help her however I could—she could have come to me—she was Harriet's mother, after all."

"When did you see her last, Mr. Cooper?" asked Hackett.

"A week ago Friday night, when I went to pick up Harriet after work. It was about seven-thirty. She—she seemed just like her usual self."

Mrs. Cooper came back with Harriet. Harriet looked a good deal happier today, an attractive, neat child in a pretty blue Sunday dress, more color in her face. Mendoza took her gently through it again, and it came out just the same. She'd gone to bed on Thursday night before Mama came home, she hadn't awakened or heard any noise, and she always got up and fixed her own breakfast, it wasn't till she came home from school she noticed Mama was still in bed.

Hackett asked her, "Do you know if she used to have something to drink before she went to bed? Something to help her fall asleep?"

Her grave eyes were thoughtful on him. "I guess she did sometimes. I sort of remember she said about it to Jerry. How it sort of helped settle her down when she was charged up."

"Jerry," said Mendoza. "Jerry Wall? Did he come to see her often?"

"Just when they were going out someplace, like a movie or something."

"Do you like him?"

"Oh, he's okay," said Harriet indifferently.

Cooper came out to the front porch with them. He said, "I suppose—I get custody automatically now? I hope so. But I just don't understand at all how it happened."

Mendoza switched on the ignition and Hackett said, "Well, that was a little exercise in futility. Why didn't you ask him where he was on Thursday night?"

"*Obvio, amigo.* He'd say, right here at home. Possibly his mother goes to bed early, but if she knew he'd been out she wouldn't tell us."

"Well, he had a motive of sorts—now he can keep his whole paycheck—but, Luis, how in hell could he have done it? If he'd been at the apartment the kid would have known, have heard him—"

"Not necessarily," said Mendoza. "He could have been waiting for her to come home, and gone upstairs with her—no need to ring the bell. And suggested a drink—made some excuse—she wouldn't have suspected anything—"

"So she stood and watched him spike hers with the phenobarbital?"

58

"Now, Art. There are ways it could have been done, if you stop and think. Just at random, he could have said he needed her Social Security number for some insurance form—I'll bet you he's got his insurance made out to Harriet—and she wasn't a very smart girl, she'd swallow any story he gave her. And he fixed the drinks while she went to get her handbag—"

"You had her just coming home, she'd have had it right there handy. He seems like a perfectly straight citizen, doesn't strike me as a killer."

"Maybe so," said Mendoza, sounding dissatisfied. "But I'll have to agree with the witnesses we've heard—an empty-headed, shallow little female like that never turned into a suicide."

About a quarter of one, when Higgins and Glasser had just got back from an early lunch, a rather surprising report had just come up from R. and I. The routine query Mendoza had sent in on the M.O., the man with the Doberman, had turned up one other instance, last January out in the Sheriff's Department beat in West Hollywood.

"Oh, hell," said Higgins. "There's probably nothing at all to get, but somebody'll have to talk to these people." They hadn't dropped on any of the four possibles they were hunting, but had a lead to one now through his former P.A. officer. Glasser went out on that alone, and Higgins, after calling to find out if they were home, drove out to West Hollywood to see Mr. and Mrs. Robert Albrecht.

They were ordinary solid citizens, just slightly more affluent than average; he was a C.P.A. They remembered the occasion vividly, and told Higgins about it at length. They'd been on their way home from a visit to Albrecht's sister in Hollywood, it was about eight-thirty one Saturday night, and they'd stopped at a drugstore to get cigarettes, a few other odds and ends. Just by chance they'd parked around on a side street, pretty dark, down from Santa Monica Boulevard; and when they came back to the car, this man was walking toward them. With the dog. "A great big thing, one of these

Doberman pinschers," said Albrecht. "I don't mind most dogs but I'm always leery of them. I was just unlocking the car when he came up, and all of a sudden he stopped, and looked at us, and then he said, 'Excuse me.' "

"What?" said Higgins.

"That's right, he said, 'Excuse me, but this is a trained attack dog and I'll set him at you unless you hand over your money.' "

"And?"

"Well, Betty let out a scream and told me for goodness' sake not to argue—"

"I've always been scared of big dogs," she confessed. "And it was so sudden—"

"How much did you give him?"

"I didn't have much on me, lucky for us. About twelve dollars. And he just took off, walking kind of fast, and we got in the car. I couldn't give you much of an idea what he looked like—it was damned dark on the side street. He was about five eleven, just a shape, had a hat on—tell you the truth, Sergeant, I was watching the dog more than I was him."

"A horrible big brute it was," she said with a shiver. "It had a head just like a snake. I was petrified."

Just as Higgins had foreseen, that presented no lead to the enterprising heister with the Doberman.

Mendoza had gone home, and Hackett was alone in the office at a little past two o'clock; Landers and Grace had brought in a possible suspect and were closeted in an interrogation room. When Lake buzzed him, it was a Sergeant Tolliver of the Bakersfield force. "Sorry to have taken a while to get back to you, but we've been a little busy. This Bussard."

"What?" said Hackett, and then made the connection. "Oh, yes." Those bodies yesterday—Glasser had been on it, but he wasn't around now. "What have you turned up?"

"Nothing. The address you had, nobody there knows him. But there are a couple of Bussards listed in the city directory. You like us to follow it up and ask them?"

"We'll return the favor some day. It just looks like a straight murder-suicide, but we'd like to get it cleared up, and not stick the taxpayers for a funeral unless it's necessary."

"Okay, we'll get to it as soon as we can and get back to you."

"Thanks so much," said Hackett. And that reminded him of something else; he asked Lake to get him SID and asked if the morgue had sent over those slugs. It had, and the ballistics man said they were .38s. Glasser had also, of course, sent over the gun, and it was a match; the slugs were out of the old S. and W. .38. "This other one," said the ballistics man, "looks like another thirty-eight, probably a Colt of some kind. We'll get to it."

"Which other— Oh." The hospital would have sent in the bullet from Price.

"You'll get a report."

Lake buzzed him again and said, "You've got a new corpse."

"Oh, hell and damnation," said Hackett. "Where?"

Palliser came in just as he was leaving, and tagged along.

It was a little street you'd never suspect was there, tucked away off one side of a side street down from Echo Park Avenue. Its name was Hope Lane. It was a dead-end street, with only six houses on each side: little modest old houses, stucco and frame, on standard city lots. The black-and-white was in front of the house last but one on the right side. As Hackett pulled up behind it and they got out, the street was very quiet; nothing stirred anywhere. Nobody seemed to have noticed the presence of the squad, or to feel curious about it.

The patrolman was Ray Waring; he was waiting on the sidewalk beside the squad, talking to a woman. "It's in the back yard," he told Hackett and Palliser. "This is Mrs. Coffman, she found him and called in."

She was, they saw instantly, ghoulishly and gleefully pleased at her role in the affair. She was about fifty, neither fat nor thin, round-faced, dowdily dressed in blouse and skirt and run-over flat oxfords. Her pale-blue eyes glittered at them pleasedly as Waring mentioned their names.

"Pleased to meet you, I'm sure. The house was unlocked so I just called from there. I never had such a shock in my life." If that was so, she'd gotten over it fast. "You see, how it was, he owed me twenty dollars. I came in and cleaned for him when he couldn't stand it any longer—how that man hated to part with money. I'd been here on Wednesday afternoon doing the windows and such, and when he got home he said he hadn't been to the bank, he'd pay me later. I dropped into the store to remind him—"

"What store?" asked Palliser.

"He had a pharmacy on Alvarado. He was a pharmacist. And yesterday he said if I dropped by today he'd pay me. That man. The bank charges for checks, he didn't like to use them. Just putting it off—a real miser he was—but he always paid in the end. And when he didn't answer the bell, I naturally figured he was in the back yard, he was quite a gardener, always working out there, about his only interest—so I went down the drive and there he was. Dead," she said enjoyably. "All bashed around—somebody had it in for him good."

Hackett exchanged a glance with Waring. "All right, Mrs. Coffman, if you wouldn't mind waiting a few minutes we may want to ask you some questions."

"I don't mind at all."

They went down the narrow drive. The house was an old frame bungalow painted white with green trim, very neat. There was about twelve feet between its side and, across the drive, the next house, which was a stucco pseudo-Spanish crackerbox. There wasn't a sound but their footsteps down the cracked-cement drive. The lot was probably the usual fifty by a hundred and fifty. At the end of the drive was a single frame garage, door open, with an old Ford sedan in it. Between garage and the back of the house was a white picket fence with a gate in it. The gate was open.

The back yard, perhaps forty by ninety feet, had been laid out as a garden of sorts, but not with flowers and shrubs; it consisted of neat rows with labeled stakes here and there.

There was already a little stand of green corn, and Hackett recognized the lacy tops of carrots, that was about all. The body was sprawled out just in front of the rows of corn. They went closer and looked at it.

It was the body of a man somewhere in his fifties, a thin stringy-necked man wearing ragged old trousers and a dirty white shirt. He had a bald spot on top of his head. And he had obviously sustained a savage beating, and died of it. His face was heavily bruised and battered, his nose mashed to one side, and there were darkening bruises on his bare arms, undoubtedly a lot more on the body.

Hackett bent and felt him. "Cold. It didn't just happen. Four or five hours maybe."

"Doesn't look as if there'll be anything for the lab, but you never know."

"We do have to go by the rules." The man had apparently been weeding the garden; there was a long-handled hoe half under the body, nothing else around. But the encounter had, also obviously, happened right here; there were a lot of scuff marks in the loosened soil, several plants uprooted and wilting, some blood spatters, what looked like a knocked-out tooth.

"It's funny," said Palliser, "that nobody found him before. Right out in the open." He looked at the house next door. On that side of the driveway there was a low cement-block wall marking the property line. They could see into a neat back yard with a strip of lawn, flower beds, a garage at the other side. In the other direction, there was another white picket fence, and the next back yard was not nearly so neat: a half-hearted attempt at a lawn, and children's toys scattered around, a bicycle.

The whole neighborhood was as silent as the tomb. "Sunday," said Hackett. "People not home." They went back down the drive. Waring had Mrs. Coffman ensconced in the back of the squad. Hackett got in the front. At least he needn't be tactful with this one. "Who was he?" he asked bluntly.

"His name's George Parmenter," she said promptly. "He

owns the Independent Pharmacy up on Alvarado. Ran it for thirty years or more. His wife used to help him in the store, but she died about three-four years ago. I just live over on Laveta, go in the store all the time, and he knew I take on housework for people sometimes. Just since she died, and he was here alone, he had me come in to do the heavy work, every couple of months."

"Miser, was he?"

"Oh, my, say it twice, Sergeant."

"Would you know if he had, well, any enemies? People he'd cheated maybe, or—"

"Well, no, I wouldn't say that." She was disappointed about it. "When I say miser I mean he just squeezed every penny. I guess he was honest enough. I don't think he knew anybody well enough to have any enemies, Sergeant. Not that I knew him so good at that, but he never went anywhere but the store and home, and all his spare time he worked in his vegetable garden."

"Well, thanks. We'll want you to come in and make a statement. Tomorrow will do." She was reluctant to leave, but finally got into the old Chevy parked ahead of the squad, and drove off. Hackett put in a call for a lab truck and got out to join Palliser in the street. "This is a funny little backwater, John. Twelve houses. Hardly more than a couple of hundred feet long. And a dead end. You'd think somebody along here would have seen or heard something. Let's go ask while the lab takes pictures."

"It was probably this morning sometime. Obviously nobody heard anything or we'd have been called before. But for one thing," said Palliser, "I'd think the people along here would notice a strange car, one that didn't belong here. No harm in asking, anyway."

Hackett took the house to the right of Parmenter's, the last house on the street this side. He had to push the doorbell twice before the door opened. He produced the badge and explained economically. She was a thirtyish, attractive woman, dark-haired, casual in jeans and blouse. Her eyes widened on him, and she put a hand to her mouth.

"For heaven's sake!" she exclaimed. "Mr. Parmenter? Right next door— Oh, my goodness. That's awful."

"Have you been home all day? Do you live alone, Mrs.—"

"Hilbrand. No, of course not, yes, I have, but I haven't heard a *thing*. How *awful*. My husband took the children up to the zoo in Griffith Park, but I had one of my sinus head-aches and didn't feel like going, I took a couple of codeine tablets— My heavens. I can't get over it—right next door—"

"Did you know Mr. Parmenter well?"

"Oh, no. He wasn't very friendly with neighbors, and be-sides he was away all day in his store, you know."

Frustrated, Hackett joined Palliser two doors down. A couple of faces were peering out a front window there. Palliser said briefly, "Middle-aged couple named Klaber. Didn't notice a thing. She's been sewing all day in the den at the other side of the house, and he's been watching TV."

Hackett massaged his jaw. "Damn it, you'd think, on a street like this— It's so damned quiet."

"Isn't it?" said Palliser. "I think the strange car's the best bet. It's not a transient neighborhood, Art. The people along here would know each other's cars, casually notice a strange one—no reason to turn in here unless you were heading for one of these houses. There wouldn't be anything to worry them, just a strange car stopping at old Parmenter's place— if somebody was out working in the yard earlier today—"

They had time to kill while the lab men were busy. They split up again, across the street. On the narrow front porch of another square crackerbox, Hackett waited, and a fussy voice inside said, "I'm coming, I'm coming—yes?" The door was opened halfway, suspiciously. She was a stout elderly woman with frizzy white hair. He explained. She was alarmed, outraged, indignant. "Why, that's just terrible! To think of that poor man— No, I just knew him to speak to, but he'd lived here a long time, of course—such a respectable man, too— But this has always been such a quiet street, I don't recall we've ever had a burglary or even any vandalism along here, but these days . . ." Her name was Helen Lewis, and she was a widow who lived alone. "I haven't heard a thing all day, it's been a very quiet day. I was in the kitchen a good part of the morning, mixing up that casserole, and I always take a little nap after lunch—"

Hackett joined Palliser. "Couple in the seventies there—Mr. and Mrs. Sadler. They were doing yard work in the back all morning. He's a little deaf."

"Helpful," said Hackett.

"Well, there's only seven more houses up to the cross street." The lab truck had arrived, and Waring gone back on tour.

They proceeded on. Hackett talked to a youngish husband and wife named Anderson, who had been refinishing furniture in their garage and hadn't heard or seen anything unusual. To a stout spinster named Spooner who had been reading in her bedroom all day. To another middle-aged couple named Trask who had been watching old movies on TV. They were all horrified and alarmed at the news, asked questions and exclaimed, but none of them had any scrap of information to offer, and none of them had known Parmenter except by sight; he hadn't been very neighborly, they said.

At the other end of the street he pushed the last doorbell. The door opened suddenly and he faced a large man with a cheerful Irish-looking bulldog face. Hackett recited the tale again. "For God's sake!" said the man. "Old Parmenter? I'll be damned!"

"If you happened to notice a strange car around, anything unusual, Mr.—"

"Branagan, Terence. I haven't noticed a damned thing, Sergeant," he said regretfully. "Fact is, I'm usually bushed on Sunday. I walk a damned long mail route, and come Sunday I just want to relax. My wife took the kids over to her mother's, and I've been half asleep in front of the tube, tell the truth. And all the time a thing like that going on." He went on to ask eager questions, and Hackett cut him off, walked across to join Palliser.

66

"One young couple named Jepson," said Palliser, "who say the baby kept them awake all night and when they got her settled down they went back to bed again, about ten A.M. He's got enough muscles to beat anybody to death, he drives a cab for Yellow and looks like a prizefighter, but I don't suppose he's our boy. Another couple about thirty-five, the Kellers, who've been painting a back bedroom all day. And a deaf widower named Weekes."

"Oh, for God's sake," said Hackett. A deathly hush lay over the little street; it was so quiet that they could hear a couple of mourning doves in the old elm tree in front of Parmenter's house the length of the street away. The morgue wagon was there now. "Well, the only answer is, he must have been knocked unconscious right away, didn't have a chance to fight back or make any noise."

"Yes," said Palliser. "I suppose we'd better have a look through the house. There may be some lead to whoever hated him enough for that."

There wasn't. Marx and Fisher were in the house now, being thorough, but it was the barest house Hackett had ever seen. There was a minimum of furniture, linen, dishes, a meagerly stocked refrigerator: not a book in the place, no desk, no visible correspondence. "He was a hermit," said Palliser.

"There may be something at the store," said Hackett. "Some people must have known him, John."

"Somebody knew him well enough to want him dead."

It was nearly the end of shift. They had Parmenter's keys from his pants pocket, and told the lab men to lock up after themselves.

Late Sunday afternoon, as Mendoza was reading in a corner of the living room, he heard Alison come in with the twins and chase them upstairs to Mairí for their baths. They departed noisily comparing the virtues of the ponies, and Alison came wandering in with Cedric and sat down opposite him. Cedric flopped down at her feet, panting loudly. Her hair was a little disheveled and she was looking meditative.

"They're getting to be quite good little riders," she said.

"Fine," said Mendoza.

"But," said Alison uneasily, "Ken says eventually we'll have to get a horse."

"¡No me diga! ¿Para qué es esto? Why a horse? They won't be six until August."

"Well, it's fine right now, but they're not going to be satisfied forever just riding around the ring, Luis. As they get more experienced they're going to want to take the ponies up in the hills, and of course Ken will have to go with them. He says just a quiet old nag of some sort, it needn't cost much. And he can add on room in the stable if he can get the lumber.

"¡Por Dios!" said Mendoza.

"He still hasn't located anybody to shear the sheep, he's been asking all the vets around. After all, nobody keeps sheep in L.A."

"Nobody but us, fools that we are."

"And, Luis, do you know that those ponies have finished another ten bales of hay? And the price it's gone to—"

Mendoza regarded her with cynical amusement. "Don't say it, one thing leading to—"

"Well, it seems to."

"Hay," said Mendoza. "Sheep. A horse. My God, what next?"

The night watch didn't get a call until nine o'clock, and then the desk called up an attempted homicide. Conway and Piggott went out on it.

It was a small apartment building on Marview Street, and Patrolman Bill Moss was waiting for them. "Where the hell are the paramedics? I called fifteen minutes ago—the girl's lost some blood."

"What's it look like?" asked Conway.

"Rape and stabbing. The roommate just came home and found her. Marcia Currier—the victim, I mean. The roommate's Evelyn Frost. She was at the beach with her boy friend all day. She says somebody must have broken in, but there's no sign of it—"

"Oh, wait for it," said Conway. "Where?"

"Apartment D upstairs."

They took the stairs fast. Apartment D was at the end of the upper hall; the door was open. In the middle of a small, brightly furnished living room there was a girl crumpled on the floor with a lot of blood around her, and another girl bending over her crying. She was a pretty, dark girl; the one on the floor was blond. She looked up wildly. "Where's the ambulance? Are you—"

"Police. It'll be along. What do you know about this, is it Miss Frost?"

"Yes, yes—nothing—I just found her—oh, Marcia darling —I can't imagine—we're both careful about keeping doors locked, and she'd never let a stranger in—he must have broken in—"

"Has she said anything at all, has she been conscious since you found her?"

"Yes, but it didn't mean anyth— She was t-trying to get up when I came in, she said my name— *Where's the ambulance?*"

"Anything else?"

She brushed back her hair, straightening up. "I don't think she was all the way conscious, didn't know what she was— Queer, she said something like *Jekyll and Hyde*—"

"Oh, my sweet Christ!" said Conway disgustedly. "Dapper Dan. That's right, it's Sunday." And then the paramedics arrived, and took the girl out in a hurry, and the Frost girl went with them.

Piggott looked at the bloodstains lugubriously. "Like the children of Israel," he said.

"What the hell?"

"Bricks without straw. He's hit, let's see, this is the ninth time, and the lab's never picked up a trace of him on any of them."

"There's always a first time. I'll get a unit out." Conway started back downstairs to the squad.

Piggott looked around sadly. The devil, these days, was getting out and around and accomplishing too much.

Monday was Palliser's day off. This would be a big day for Nick Galeano, who hadn't shown up yesterday at all; and it remained to be seen how many of the men at Robbery-Homicide, who'd worked with him for a good many years, could snatch the time to attend the wedding.

Hackett had just finished telling Mendoza about Parmenter when the hospital called to tell them that Ken Price had died during the night. One more homicide to work. Hackett looked grim as he put the phone down and passed that on. Higgins, Grace, Glasser, Landers had hung around to hear about the new one. "Ballistics said the slug was a thirty-eight, a Colt of some sort. Did that pharmacist make any mug shots, George?"

"Nary a one, but you can't take it for granted he would. When people are scared and nervous they don't always see straight. He liked a couple of the pictures the computers turned up, said that was the type—big, brawny, and mean. One Leonard Osterberg, Ernest Docker, both counts of heists and violence. We haven't dropped on them yet, but Osterberg's former P.A. officer gave us a lead on him."

"And now this damned rapist pulling another one. I wonder how the girl is."

"I called when I saw Matt's report," said Mendoza. "She'll be all right. We can probably talk to her sometime today."

"And we know what she's going to tell us," said Landers disgustedly.

"That Coffman woman's coming in to make a statement," said Hackett. "We ought to have a look around Parmenter's store, see if any leads show there. I wonder if he hired any help. And we ought to get the autopsy report on Cooper today—"

"Also anonymous," said Mendoza. "We seem to be getting them."

"We never talked to her boy friend."

"You have to wait for the Coffman woman. I'll do that," said Mendoza, "and the rest of you have places to go. *Vamos and buena suerte.*"

"Look, I'm damn sorry about it but I don't know one damn thing about it," said Jerry Wall.

"So you won't mind answering a few questions," said Mendoza placidly. He had found Wall at the garage on Vermont where he worked, and Wall had reluctantly taken him into the closet-sized cluttered office of the owner.

"Listen, I didn't even know about it till I went to pick up Marion on Friday night, this woman in the next apartment says she's dead! Look, it doesn't look so good, the fuzz come asking me questions—Mr. Nolan's due back from the bank anytime—"

"Anybody can be acquainted with a suicide," said Mendoza, getting out a cigarette.

Wall looked at him uncertainly. He was rather obviously good-looking, a husky six-footer with overlong sandy-blond hair, a boyish face that ended in a narrow weak jaw. Mendoza put him around thirty-two or -three, but he looked younger: only the faint lines at eye corner and mouth gave him away. Like Landers, thought Mendoza amusedly, forever being told he didn't look old enough for a detective; but that was a matter of shape and structure, and there was nothing weak about Tom's long jaw. "Did she kill herself?" asked Wall. "That woman didn't know much."

"Why, were you expecting her to be murdered?" asked Mendoza, trickling smoke through his nostrils.

"Well, for God's sake, no! How should I know what happened?"

"You were the steady boy friend, you'd know how she'd been feeling lately."

"She never said anything— Only for a while," he said sullenly. He hadn't sat down, leaned against the wall; his white T-shirt clung to his broad torso. "She had some other ones."

"At the moment I'm interested in you. Where did you get together to make out?"

"Listen, it wasn't nothing like that, Marion was a nice girl—I—we really hadn't been goin' together very long—"

"Oh, now, come on," said Mendoza. "Give us the credit for some sense, Wall. I'm not going to swallow a tale that you took her out to a movie and bought her an ice-cream soda and kissed her good night at the door. Nobody's accusing you of anything, I just want the facts."

"Oh, for Christ's sake!" said Wall roughly. "So all right, all right, there wasn't anything in it, see? Neither of us wanted to get hooked up again—at least I was lucky not to come in for the alimony, I could show the judge Marie was a lush and a tramp—but like you say, we wasn't kids, for God's sake. It didn't mean one damn thing, see? Like—like—" he cast around in his mind, and said ingenuously, "Like—one for the road. Just the good time."

Mendoza eyed him thoughtfully, understanding that to perfection. The careless good time. No, it wouldn't have mattered much to either of them; and that, of course, was what was basically wrong with it. There had been a time when Luis Mendoza had subscribed to that simple philosophy too; only a fortuitous set of circumstances—and another rapist— had put more understanding in him.

"Yes," he said, and stabbed out his cigarette. "Did you use her place?"

"My God, no. I was getting fed up, it was a damn nuisance, see. She was always so goddamned nervous about her ex, on account of the alimony and the support for the kid. She was scared he'd get a private eye on her, get the kid away so he wouldn't have to pay her. I told her it was silly, he couldn't afford nothing like that—but she wouldn't let me come to her place except to pick her up—and she wouldn't go in my place either—"

"Back of the car," said Mendoza.

"I was fed up. Look, Marion was a nice enough girl but she wasn't the only one around, see? And for God's sake, I don't know what happened to her. Last time I saw her was at the coffee shop Wednesday, she looked just like usual, I said I'd pick her up Friday night."

"And where were you Thursday night?" Mendoza didn't think it mattered.

"For God's sake. It was a kind of rough day, I was beat. I shot a little pool down the block, and I had dinner at a joint and went home and went to bed."

Mendoza had lost interest in him three minutes ago. He stood up.

He got to the church in good time; it was St. Joseph's up on Vermont. There wasn't much of a crowd, maybe twenty-five people; Nick would have relations, but the bride didn't have any family in this country. Palliser and his Roberta were there, in a pew opposite; they hadn't noticed Mendoza yet, and he sat back thinking about that old case when he'd half suspected Roberta of a rather complicated murder. They were a distinguished-looking pair, both tall, dark and handsome.

Hackett slid into the pew beside him just as the organ music changed and the bride appeared. Landers and Grace had gone down the side aisle at the same time.

It was a simple low mass, without more music or much ritual. He hadn't seen the bride since he'd seriously suspected her of murdering her first husband. He hadn't remembered that she was such a good-looking girl: loose-waved tawny-blond hair, the warm dark eyes, a milky complexion. She was wearing a simple beige dress. And stocky dark Galeano, that staid bachelor, even managed to look the romantic bridegroom, in a formal dark suit. The blinding smile they exchanged at the end of the ceremony maybe meant more than the ritual. And when the reception line formed outside, there was a cluster of pretty plump dark women around bride and groom—Galeano's mother and sisters.

The Pallisers had gotten there first, and the bride was talking animatedly to Roberta when Mendoza offered congratulations to Galeano. "Marta," he said, and she turned quickly.

"All the best wishes, Mrs. Galeano."

Her dark eyes held a smile. "Lieutenant Mendoza, who was so convinced I had murdered my poor husband. Thank you."

"You'd better not murder this one," said Mendoza. "We're shorthanded as it is."

She laughed. "I promise you will have him back in two little weeks—and with the five pounds lost he has gained! I will take care of him for you."

Mendoza moved on, and a minute later on the way to the parking lot Glasser caught up to him and said, "Another confirmed bachelor caught in the trap."

"You're just a cynic, Henry."

FOUR

When Higgins and Landers had gotten to the Independent Pharmacy on Alvarado that morning, they had found a woman peering in the front window, looking at the *Closed* sign on the door. Getting out the keys he had from Hackett, Higgins said, "I'm sorry, ma'am, the store won't be open today."

"Oh," she said. "I wondered why Mr. Parmenter wasn't here, it's after nine. Is he sick? Who are you?"

"I'm sorry to tell you he's died. Did you know him, ma'am?" Higgins unlocked the door.

"Died! Well, for goodness' sake," she said mildly. She was a dumpy, dowdy woman in the forties, with lank brown hair, a homely plain face. "So I guess I'm out of a job."

"You worked here?"

"Just since last week. It must have been awful sudden, he seemed all right on Saturday."

Higgins produced the badge and brought her in, to save time letting her think it had been an accident of some kind. Her name was Amelia Bowler and she said she'd answered an ad in the *Times* last Tuesday, there'd been a number to call, and Mr. Parmenter had hired her right away when he told her the address and she came. "He said the other clerk he'd had had left all of a sudden and he needed somebody. I was glad to get the job even if it didn't pay much, we can use the extra money since my husband's been sick and off work." She looked around the shabby old store regretfully. "And an easy job, just waiting on people. I'm sure sorry to hear about Mr. Parmenter—he was kind of quiet and a little crabby, but you got to take people as you find them." She didn't know anything about the other clerk.

Higgins let her out and looked around the store, which was old and run-down and cluttered; this was a block of tired old businesses, a cleaners', a cut-rate dress shop, a hole-in-the-wall doughnut shop, a music store offering LP records below cost. Landers was poking around in the back room. Higgins went behind the counter at the rear of the store and found the phone in a little dispensing office there. He called the office.

"Art? Is that Coffman woman still there? Well, would you ask her . . ."

After an interval Hackett reported, "She was surprised to hear the other clerk had quit her job. Says she'd been there about four years, since Parmenter's wife died. Coffman hadn't been in the store for about two weeks, so she didn't know she'd left. She's not sure about the woman's name but it was Mac something, she thinks."

They looked around, in all the drawers and files in the stockroom, but there didn't seem to be any correspondence, either business or private; nothing but a shabby store, a clutter of stock this sort and that, cosmetics, a little stationery, a tobacco counter, men's shaving lotion and razor blades, all the miscellany expectable in such a place. "It's a funny one," said Landers, "by what Art said. Nothing much to get hold of."

"This other woman probably knew something about him, working here that long." They looked further and found some boxes of canceled checks on a shelf in the storeroom; among them were checks made out to Alice McLennan, all in the

76

amount of four hundred and fifty dollars. "Piddling salary," commented Higgins. "This is probably her." The checks were drawn on a Bank of America five blocks down Alvarado, and marked for deposit only. "So she's got an account there too. Let's see if we can locate her."

At the bank, the badges produced cooperation. Miss Alice McLennan was one of their depositors, and her address was on Baxter Street.

It was an ancient eight-unit apartment, and she lived at the front upstairs. There was no response to the bell, and Higgins said, "Working-class neighborhood. She won't be rich—she'll have gotten herself another job. Maybe somebody here will know where."

Downstairs, the left front door bore a sign, *Manageress.* The woman who answered that bell was pleasant-faced, politely helpful. "Miss McLennan, well, she's gone off for a little vacation. Somewhere up in the mountains, she said. She said she'd be back next week sometime. Well, I couldn't say exactly where. Now Mrs. Bickerstaff might know, she lives across the hall from Miss McLennan and they're great friends, but of course she's gone to stay with her daughter, help with the sick baby, and I don't know when she might be home— it's someplace in West Covina, I don't know the address."

"I see," said Higgins. "Well, we're anxious to talk to Miss McLennan. It's about her former employer. I wonder, when you do see her, if you'd ask her to call this number. Or if Mrs. Bickerstaff comes back—"

"Oh, surely," she said amiably, taking the card. "Business of some kind. I know she'd just quit her job. She said she really needed a vacation, and she just took Mickey and drove off to the mountains. Somewhere."

"Mickey."

"Her little fox terrier. She's just crazy about that dog—a nice little dog."

"And so," said Higgins, "unless she can tell us something, I wouldn't know where to go on it. There aren't any personal effects at the store, no correspondence. It looks as if the place hadn't been cleaned much or straightened out in years." It was after four-thirty; he and Grace had stayed on at the wedding reception.

"It didn't look as if the house had been entered at all," said Hackett, taking his glasses off to polish them. "Scarne called just before I left last night. They came across a thousand bucks in cash in one of the kitchen canisters—"

"*¡Como!*" said Mendoza. "First place a burglar would look. He was supposed to be a shrewd miser?"

"It shapes up," said Hackett, breathing on his glasses and polishing absently, "that somebody just drove up there, spotted him in the back yard, walked down and beat him to a pulp. And they can't have made much noise, none of the neighbors heard a thing. That's a damned queer little backwater of a place, tucked away like that. They were all home too, but it was natural enough, all of them had reasons why they weren't noticing anything, everybody—so to speak—doing their own thing, on a nice quiet Sunday. But there's just nowhere to go on it if we can't get a line on the people he knew. Damn it, there wasn't even an address book at the house."

"Or the store," said Higgins.

"This former employee may give us something."

"Mmh, yes," said Mendoza, "a shapeless little thing. And it'll be a day or two before we get an autopsy report." He picked up the manila folder from his desk blotter. "What we have got, just now, is the autopsy report on Marion Cooper." He sat back and lit a new cigarette, and blew smoke at the ceiling. At this end of a day, he needed a shave, but looked as sharply tailored and neat as when he'd left home, the tie tidily centered, correct quarter inch of cuff showing. "And what it tells us is, the fatal old combination of pills and booze. She'd had about six drinks—scotch and soda—and something like fifteen phenobarbital capsules, and *terminar*. I suppose we'll get a lab report on that apartment sometime, they do take their time. And she'd had sexual intercourse fairly recently before death."

"Oh," said Hackett alertly, and sat up. "Wall?"

"I really don't think so, Art. He's the simple male animal, there is no guile in him. I think he was telling me the truth." Mendoza brooded over the manila folder. "She wasn't promiscuous, I don't think, but—the good-time girl. It didn't mean that much to her." He thought that over, and added, "Maybe she'd have gotten down to being promiscuous in another couple of years. As it was, Wall said she had other boy friends. Maybe she ran into an old flame that night, at one of those bars."

"Yes," said Hackett, "we haven't looked at those yet, have we? Well, a job for the night watch." He stood up and stretched. "At least we've got Nick safely married off. Nice wedding—pretty girl. I just hope we don't get a spate of business while we're shorthanded."

"Don't invite trouble," said Higgins. "We're overdue for a heat wave, and that always sends the homicide rate up."

Whether they got called out or not, the night watch would be busy, the day men leaving jobs for them—on Dapper Dan's latest victim, the new homicide. Piggott said, "I'll go to the hospital. You can go barhopping." Piggott was, of course, a teetotaler.

At the hospital, of course, he heard exactly what he'd expected to hear from Marcia Currier. She was sitting up in bed looking a little pale, but otherwise all right, and Evelyn Frost was there. "Honestly," said Marcia, "honestly! I didn't hesitate a minute—he was so polite and apologetic for bothering me, he seemed so worried about his sister, it was all so plausible and, well, I mean, broad daylight, about four o'clock on Sunday afternoon! I didn't even have time to scream—"

She offered the expectable description. Tall, dark, clean shaven, early thirties, the nicely tailored suit, white shirt and tie. She said she'd be glad to come in and look at mug shots.

Piggott, either because or in spite of his religious convictions, tended to be a pessimist; this time he had solid reason. Almost certainly Marcia Currier wasn't going to pick out any mug shots.

Conway and Schenke hit Barney's Bar and Grill first, and ran into some pay dirt, but meager. It was a typical third-class bar, the dim lighting disguising the shabbiness of the cheaply upholstered booths, the scratched and stained tables, even the ill-adjusted TV suspended in one corner. It was noisy and friendly. They talked to the bartender and he pointed out some regulars he remembered Marion fraternizing with: a young couple who said sure, they dropped in here a few nights a week, and sure, they knew Marion. They were shocked to hear she was dead. They pointed out a pair of men they'd seen her sitting with: Conway and Schenke talked to them. Bill Voorhees, Joe Otero: they were frank, shocked, puzzled, unhelpful. She'd seemed like a nice girl; they'd just talked with her in here, neither had ever dated her. They shared an apartment a couple of blocks away; they were both orderlies at the Beverly Glen Hospital. And everybody said that Marion hadn't been in here on Thursday night.

"Around and around we go," said Schenke philosophically. "I hope that hair-trigger heister isn't out again."

Conway just growled. His best girl worked nine to five, and he hadn't even seen her in two months. They went a block up to the Ace-High Bar, which was a replica of Barney's except that it was bigger and had color TV. There, they found the barmaid who had known Marion. Her name was Amy Hall. She was astonished to hear about Marion, not apparently especially grieved; she said readily that, yeah, Marion had been in last Thursday night. She'd left earlier than usual. Before that she'd been talking with a couple of the regulars, and they were here now; she pointed out two women sitting at a small table alone. Conway and Schenke went over and showed the badges.

That pair stuck out as homosexuals: one hard-faced female in a pantsuit, with an offhand manner and cold eyes, one vacant-eyed giggler. They said indifferently they knew Marion, and she'd been here last Thursday. The giggler said, "She left with that Italiano guy, I think they said something about going somewhere to dance. Oh, his name's Galloopsi or something. I only heard it once."

They went back to the barmaid. "Oh," she said, "well, I didn't notice if she left with anybody—I just saw her waving at me from the door, and it was early, about nine o'clock. What? Well, I guess she'd had about three scotches, the time she was here, call it from seven on. An Italian guy? That could be Tony Galluci, she knew him, sure."

"Do you know where he works, lives?"

She laughed. "He's one of the custodians up at the Police Academy in Elysian Park. I got no idea where he lives."

"Well, for God's sake," said Conway outside. He took a grateful breath of night air, out of the steamy atmosphere at the Ace-High. "That's a little switch. Shall we leave the rest of it to the day men?"

Bob Schenke yawned. "Night's still fairly young. Let's work it a little more, Rich."

The academy, of course, was shut down for the night, but most people had phones. They found him in the Central book, over on Burnside Avenue above Olympic. It was an old apartment building, and he was at home. He was around thirty, superficially handsome with a dark narrow face and patent-leather hair. At least he was very much at ease with police, rubbing shoulders with them every day.

He was surprised to hear about Marion; he said several times he'd be good and damned; he was sorry, she'd been a fun girl. Not that he'd known her very well, he'd only dated her a couple of times.

"Including," said Conway, "last Thursday night."

"Yeah, that's right. I ran into her at the Ace-High, we had a few drinks, and then she had a yen to go dancing somewhere. We went to a place out on Olympic that has a combo, but of course we both had to go to work next day, I guess it was about a quarter of twelve I dropped her off at her place. No, I didn't go in with her."

"But you'd already had a heavy necking session in the car, hadn't you? And I do mean heavy," said Conway.

Galluci wasn't annoyed or embarrassed at all. "Yeah, that's right. So what, it's a free country. Matter of fact it was the first time, like I say it was only the third time I'd been out with her. It's a shame, her dying like that—she was a real fun girl."

Mendoza uttered a sharp laugh and pushed Conway's report across the desk to Hackett and Higgins. "*¿Pues y qué?* I really don't see any reason for Galluci to want to murder Marion—just the easy lay. The more you look at it, it's a very queer setup."

"I don't suppose Cooper could be right?" said Hackett. "An accident of some sort—it'd be the simple explanation. If she took a last drink to settle her down, reached for the aspirin without turning on the light—if she had that stuff around—" He stopped.

"Don't gibber, *chico*," said Mendoza. He brushed his mustache back and forth irritably. "About fifteen capsules? And it was in the scotch."

"Yes, I just remembered that."

"Well, I want to look around that pharmacy some more. I had one thought, Luis. When Parmenter was said to be so greedy for money, it could be he'd been dealing in the pills—he could acquire the stuff all legal. And any unusual amounts might show on his books."

"*Posible*," said Mendoza. "It would also probably be known in the neighborhood. To, I needn't tell you, the kids. You can go and ask."

Everybody else was out hunting heisters. On impulse, after Hackett and Higgins left, he went downstairs and drove over to take a look at the funny little backwater. Hope Lane. It was quiet as death, all right. Just the twelve little houses, looking prim and somnolent in the early sun. At the very end, at the house next to Parmenter's, a dark young woman was out working in a front flower bed. She looked curiously at the Ferrari as he turned around in the dead end.

He came back to the office and reread Conway's report. It conveyed nothing new to him. He went down the hall for coffee, and was rereading the autopsy report on Marion when Sergeant Lake buzzed him.

"They want somebody down in Echo Park," he said. "I don't know on what. There are a couple of squads there now."

"*¿Qué es esto?*" Resignedly Mendoza got up, automatically yanking down his cuffs, and picked up the Homburg. "Don't tell me there's a body in the lake."

"They didn't say." Lake had temporarily given up his diet, and was bulging slightly in his uniform. He looked bored, picking up his paperback.

Echo Park wasn't that much of a park: call it eight or nine acres, and most of it the lake; and it didn't attract the custom it once had. There were boats to rent, little putt-putt motor boats with canvas tops, but such unsophisticated pursuits were no longer popular with the younger generation, and there wasn't much else there but a hamburger stand, pretty scenery around the edge of the lake.

You couldn't drive into the park; he parked in a red zone along Echo Park Avenue and walked down. There were two squads in a red zone down from there, and down the little slope, past one of the cement paths leading into the park, were two uniformed men standing at the shore of the lake under a big pine tree.

As he started toward them, he remembered that body in the lake, some while ago. An offbeat case. Occasionally they came along.

The two uniformed men were Barrett and Zimmerman. It was probably Gomez's day off. "I don't know if you'll think we handled this right, Lieutenant," said Barrett, looking disturbed. "But we didn't want to call you out unless there was really something to it, you see, and so we did a little looking on our own. I called for a backup because—well, it could be something and then again it couldn't, see what I mean. But we both think now there damn well could be something to it. Look at this." He gestured. "The fellow who runs the boat concession spotted it, when he came to open up about ten A.M."

Under the tree, on the largely bare earth where grass wouldn't spread in the deep shade, was a little collection of objects. There was a large green canvas tote bag, with a ball of green wool spilling out of its top, and a pair of white-framed sunglasses lay near the wool. A foot or so away from the bag was a half-knitted green sweater, with a pair of knitting needles still in it where the last stitches had been taken. All around the area in front of the bag, near to the solid thick trunk of the tree, were little scuffle marks in the bare earth; and on the bag itself was a large splotch of blood—a good deal of blood trailing out on the canvas in a series of little sprayed droplets from the largest splotch.

"Now that's blood," said Barrett, "and not just from a nose-bleed or something. It kind of looks as if there'd been a struggle of some kind here, would you say?"

"I might," said Mendoza, looking at the exhibits with interest.

"Well, I tried not to disturb it, but I looked in the bag. There's just a handkerchief and some Life Savers in it, and there was this." He handed over a letter. It was in an envelope addressed to Miss Eileen Mooney at an address on Clinton Street. "It's just a little note from some girl thanking her for a birthday present, but the address—it's just up in the next block, and by that time Zimmerman was here so we both went up to look. No answer, and we talked to a neighbor, a Mrs. Lally. It's a four-unit place, this apartment is downstairs left, and this other downstairs tenant knows the girls. Sisters, Rose and Eileen Mooney—and she says Rose is at work but Eileen came down to the park this morning to sit and knit, about eight-thirty. She hasn't seen her come back. Well, in case the girl had been taken sick or something—I don't know if you think it was the right thing to do, but—I got in. I got a back

84

window open, and the place is empty, nobody there. All clean and neat."

"So this Eileen—" said Zimmerman. "That is blood, after all. And there isn't a soul down here, hasn't been while we've been here. It looks as if somebody could have, well, snatched her."

"¡Ay de mi!" said Mendoza. "I'll agree with you, something certainly happened here, boys. And I'd like to know if that's human blood. And something about Eileen. Where does the sister work?"

"Big restaurant up in Hollywood. By what the neighbor said they both work there, but different shifts." Barrett added the name.

"What's the address on Clinton? All right. There just could be something damn serious here, and I think we'll find out. One of you call up a lab unit, hand this stuff over, and tell them I want an analysis on the blood *pronto*. I'll see the sister. You might go asking around"—there were narrow residential streets adjoining the park—"whether anybody heard anything, screams—you never know."

"Okay," and Barrett started back to his squad.

"I'm glad you don't think we jumped the gun," said Zimmerman uneasily.

"No. Something happened here," repeated Mendoza, staring at the blood splotch soberly. "Maybe we got on it soon enough—we'll see. Call in anything you get to my office." He didn't lose time getting back to the Ferrari.

The restaurant where the Mooney sisters worked was a big one in the middle of Hollywood, almost opposite the Crossroads of the World shopping complex. It was a middle-priced place with a good reputation, not fancy, but very far from being a cheap joint. There was a square foyer where a cashier presided over a glass-cased counter displaying cigars, mints; the woman there was fat and gray-haired.

He waited for a couple of departing customers to get out of the way, asked for Rose Mooney, showed the badge. "It's a little family trouble. Is there anywhere I could talk to her privately?"

"I don't know." She looked around vaguely. "She's in the back dining room—through to the left."

Mendoza went back there, to a large square room past a dark bar, and accosted the first waitress he saw, neat in black-and-white uniform. "I'm looking for Rose Mooney, could you—"

"I'm Rose Mooney," she said. She was a small pert-looking young woman about twenty-five, with an uptilted nose and reddish-blond hair. She stared at the badge. "What's it about? *Police*—is something wrong with Eileen? What—"

"Is there somewhere we can talk privately?"

She said, "We're not supposed—I'm about due for a break —I guess we could—" She went and spoke to another waitress, led him to the last booth at the end of the room.

"Now, nobody wants to worry you unless there's good reason," said Mendoza, "but you'd better know what showed up a while ago." He told her about the curious little jumble of evidence in the park, the blood; she listened, breathing quickly, leaning forward.

"Oh, my God," she said. "But what could have— Yes, she went to the park—" She put both hands to her head, almost as if to hold it on. "Oh, my God. We usually work the day shift together, but Eileen's on the night shift just temporary, to oblige the manager—there's a girl off sick. So I've been leaving the car for her—not safe, taking the bus at night. I'm on eight to four, and she was on four to midnight. Just the last week. And since the weather's been so nice, she liked to walk down and sit in the park, mornings, and knit or read. She was going to this morning."

"Your neighbor saw her go."

"But what could have— Oh, God," she said suddenly, and drew a long shaky breath. "Oh, if she just hadn't had that fight with Randy! So senseless—I just thought, my God, it could be that awful Bartovic fellow! It could be—he'd been after her—"

86

"Now calm down and tell me about it straight," said Mendoza sharply.

"Oh, my God. She—she'd been going steady with Randy Penner a long while, he's a really nice guy, and crazy about her, but she had this stupid fight with him—last week—because he lost a hundred dollars at poker—and broke up with him. And this other one, Rudy Bartovic, he'd pestered her for a date before. I think she went out with him because she was still mad at Randy—it was last Friday night, her night off—but when she got home she said never again, she'd nearly gotten raped and he was mad she fought back—"

"All right. Do you know where he lives?"

"That's just it, why I thought of him, he lives right on the same block a couple of houses down—with his mother and a couple of younger brothers—and he could know about Eileen being in the park—could have seen her—"

"Now, Miss Mooney. Just to be sure about this, I'd like you to let me drive you home so you can look to see if any of her clothes are missing. We have to be sure she hasn't gone somewhere of her own volition."

"But where would she—why—"

"We have to be sure." He waited while she saw the manager, got her handbag, and took her out to the Ferrari. On the way downtown he asked, "Can you give me a description of your sister?"

"She—we look a lot alike. She's five two, she weighs a hundred and ten, her hair's the same color as mine and her eyes a little greener. She's twenty-two," said Rose wretchedly.

He parked on Clinton Street in front of the apartment. "Let's see if your car's here." It was, a middle-aged Datsun inside the locked garage. "She'd have her keys with her?"

"Well, of course. She'd lock the place when she left."

"You go and look at her clothes. I'll be back. Where does Bartovic live?" She pointed out the house a little way up the street.

He walked up there and pushed the doorbell. After an interval the door opened and a shapelessly fat woman in a dirty housedress faced him. "Is Rudy Bartovic here?" She shook her head, and he showed her the badge. "Do you know where he is?"

"Police," she said. "He's in some trouble again, maybe? But Mr. Reiner said he wouldn't do nothing if Rudy paid it back—" She looked frightened. "I'm afraid to cross him—you can't do nothing with him—he come home drunk again last night, and like to snap my head off this morning just 'cause I asked was he goin' to the employment agency—just slammed out—"

"What time?" asked Mendoza peremptorily. "Does he have a car?"

"About eight o'clock, I guess. Yeah—he just traded a couple weeks ago for a different one, I don't know what—"

When Landers and Palliser came in at one o'clock with a hot suspect for a heist, Mendoza was just putting down the phone. Hearing them, he came out and told them to stash the captive away a while. "You'd better hear about this thing. It just could be—it looks more like it the more we know—we've got an abduction and rape on our hands." He told them about Eileen. "Those patrolmen used their heads, but we were late on it, of course. This Bartovic sounds like a mean *hombre*. He's been working at a Shell station, and his ex-boss, Bill Reiner, says he lifted a hundred bucks from the register and he fired him. Says he's hot-tempered and lazy, he's glad to be shut of him, but he agreed not to charge him if Bartovic paid him back. He hasn't so far."

"And right in the same neighborhood," said Palliser, "he could have seen the girl on her way to the park."

"*Exactamente.* That place isn't crowded at any time, and at nine in the morning it'd be empty. Nobody around to hear her scream. He could have knocked her out, roughed her up a little, dragged her up to a car on the street. The sister says none of her clothes are missing. I got the lab on it fast, and they now tell us that is human blood."

"Bartovic got a pedigree?" asked Landers.

"A little one. Possession as a juvenile, attempted B. and E."

"And my God, if he's high on something God knows what he might do to her," said Palliser.

"I got the plate number from Sacramento just now—it's an old T-bird. There'll be an A.P.B. out on him in five minutes." Mendoza sat back and lit a cigarette with a little snap of his lighter. "Let's just hope we catch up to him fast."

About a quarter of two it occurred to Alison that the twins would be home presently, the school bus letting them off down the hill at the gate, and she might walk down to meet them. She'd been painting most of the day. She'd never had a real studio before, but the little room upstairs next to the master suite was really ideal space to keep an easel up and shelves for all the odds and ends. She looked at the canvas critically; she'd tried to get the view out over the hill, the twisting shapes of the old live oaks. On the whole she was fairly satisfied with it.

She went down the hall. Just up by the head of the spiral staircase she glanced into the nursery. Luisa Mary was slumbering peacefully in her crib after lunch, and Mairí was sitting by the window knitting, her spectacles on the end of her nose.

Downstairs, she had a glimpse of three of the cats—Bast, Nefertite and Sheba—in a complex tangle in Luis's armchair, sleeping off the morning's exercise. El Señor was brooding on top of the credenza in the entrance hall, his front paws folded in tightly.

It was a lovely day, not too warm but sunny and blue-skied. Smiling to herself, Alison went out the front door, and was instantly greeted by a couple of cordial *baas*. She took one look and uttered a shriek.

All the Five Graces, fat and woolly and busy, were feasting greedily on the new landscaping. One of them had nearly denuded an Italian cypress tree of its greenery as far up as a sheep could reach, two others were munching happily on hibiscus bushes and the other two were eating the lawn. Cedric was lying in the drive watching them.

"*Oh, my heavens!*" wailed Alison, and ran at them waving her hands. They didn't budge, looked at her happily. "You!" she said to Cedric. "You're supposed to be a sheepdog! Oh!" She ran up the hill toward the old winery, calling for Ken.

They both came out of the little apartment as she arrived, breathless: Kearney tall and loose-limbed, his little wife plumper than ever. "What's up?" asked Kearney.

"The sheep—eating all that expensive—landscaping," panted Alison. "Those cypress trees—a hundred dollars apiece, and the lawn—"

"Oh, dear," said Kate Kearney.

He scratched his chin. "I did a little thinking about that—should've mentioned it maybe. But there's a good deal of ground here, plenty of wild growth. Thing is, this climate's a little new to me, the long dry spell. They were happy enough with all the wild stuff, but now the rains are over it's all dried up and naturally they'd hunt for anything fresh and green."

"But we'll have to do something!"

"Yes, reckon I'd better shoo 'em into the corral while I put up a wire-and-post fence all around the house to keep 'em away from that."

"A *wire-and-post fence*—around my beautiful house!" Alison was outraged. "But it would look horrible!"

"Well, a nice white picket fence—"

"Around a Spanish ranch house?" said Alison crossly. "The only thing that would look right at all is a cement-block wall. Pierced cement blocks or something."

"Well, now," said Kearney, "that'd take a while to put up and cost quite a bit."

"I know, I know!" said Alison.

"You'd better let me put up a wire-and-post fence just temporary till you get the wall built," said Kearney.

Alison marched down the hill to meet the twins, fuming, with Cedric bouncing ahead of her. She scowled at his fat woolly rump "Sheepdog, my foot!" she muttered.

* * *

When Hackett came in at five-thirty he heard about Eileen with interest. "There's just no line on Parmenter at all, Luis. No sign of any friends or acquaintances even. On second thought it occurred to me if he was pushing pills, he wouldn't let the orders show on his books—anyway, they look perfectly ordinary. I talked to the business people along there, and they just knew him by sight."

"Yes, he seems to have kept himself to himself, as they say," said Mendoza.

"What about the hot suspect John was after? I ran into him at lunch and he said they'd just gotten a new address for him."

"Yes, they picked him up. He had an alibi," said Mendoza. "He was at his sister's wedding reception with about forty other people."

Hackett swore tiredly and got up.

Mendoza went home to hear all about the depredations of the sheep and the necessity for an expensive new concrete wall around the house.

The middle of the week was usually slow for the night watch; tonight they'd have been just as glad to be busy. They'd heard about Eileen, and they were worried about her. The squad on that beat was alerted to check the Bartovic house every so often, but there hadn't been a sign of him yet, and the A.P.B. hadn't turned him up anywhere else.

About ten o'clock Conway went down to Communications and borrowed a radio so they could monitor the Traffic calls. If he did show up they'd know it right away.

But nothing happened until eleven-thirty when the desk called up a heist. "All right, we're on it," said Conway to the phone. "Where'd you say? The—what the hell? Yes, okay."

The address was the Music Center over on Grand, and it was, of course, the man with the Doberman again. Bill Moss had hung around after he'd called in.

The victims were Mr. and Mrs. Adrian Muller, and they were annoyed and angry. He was a big fat man in expensive clothes, a prosperous-looking stockbroker; he mentioned his firm name at once, as if underlining that a man of such eminence shouldn't have such things happen. She was younger, with blue-tinted hair and a diamond necklace. They'd attended a concert here, and it had ended rather early but they'd run into some old friends and stayed talking in the lobby. So when all four of them came out, there was hardly anyone else in the parking lot, most cars gone, and the friends' car was parked nearer the exit. And when they got up to their own car, they'd heard somebody following them—

"I couldn't have been more scared of a gun," said the woman, shuddering. "I'm just terrified of those dogs, and that one looked as savage as a wild beast—"

"How much did he get, Mr. Muller?" asked Conway.

"Nearly seventy dollars, damn it. At least he gave me back my wallet." And of course neither of them could offer any description.

"Didn't he ask for your jewelry, Mrs. Muller?" She was wearing quite a lot of it, obviously valuable.

"If he had, I'd have handed it over, but no, he didn't."

"Outrageous," said Muller. "I'd like to know what you're going to do about it."

But it was a rhetorical question, and Conway didn't tell him there wasn't much they could do about it. It was a new and offbeat caper, and just no way to chase it down at all. The Mullers got into their car and drove off, and Bill Moss began to laugh.

"It's not really funny," said Conway.

"I guess not. But that's a weird one—and it's a damn funny thing how so many people are scared of the Dobes, when they'd walk up to something twice as big and say Nice doggie. Dogs are dogs, after all, and you can't generalize about breeds much. From going through the special course for working with the dogs we've got, I've acquired a theory about it. It's all on account of their ears being cropped."

"How's that again?"

"The Dobes. They get their ears cropped, the flap cut off.

It's been outlawed in England, and I wish they'd outlaw it here. But it's a funny thing, you see a Dobe with its natural ears, it's just a nice big friendly-looking dog."

Conway laughed. "You could be right. Anyway, there's not much chance of dropping on this one. Him and his savage beast."

Mendoza had left orders that he was to be called if Bartovic was picked up. But on Wednesday morning, with Hackett off, there was no news about Bartovic or Eileen at all. Bartovic's car hadn't been spotted, he hadn't come home, and his mother said she didn't know where he might be.

Cindy Hamilton had come in yesterday to look at mug shots, but of course hadn't made any. Higgins was feeling annoyed; all the immediate possibles on the hair-trigger heister had been exhausted with inconclusive results. "If you're interested," he told Mendoza, "I'm halfway convinced it was Osterberg. He's got the right record for it, and he matches the description. He's got no alibi, we just can't pin it on him without more evidence."

"The southern accent," said Mendoza.

"Oh, damn it, he could have faked it. Who said he had one? Just Burroughs, and he's not a good witness."

Mendoza looked up at him, looming over the desk; Higgins might as well have COP tattooed on his craggy face. "Forget about it and come help me scare somebody, George."

"Pleasure. Who?"

"Mrs. Bartovic."

But she wouldn't scare. She was a fairly stupid woman, and it finally became apparent that she really didn't know anything to tell them. She gave them the names of Rudy's best pals again, but they'd been checked out already with no result. The two younger brothers were just sullen.

The day wore on, and nothing much happened. One of the squads reported a body in an alley off Alameda, and Palliser went out to look at it, reported that it looked like another derelict dead of natural causes: a man about seventy, nothing on him but half a bottle of muscatel and a single dollar bill. The city would end up burying him.

Everything seemed to have come to a standstill, suddenly and unexpectedly; for once they didn't have enough to do. From experience, they knew it wouldn't last; but with Eileen to worry about, it worried them.

About three o'clock Mendoza had wandered out to the communal office where Higgins, Glasser, Grace and Wanda were fidgeting around; Wanda went down the hall and brought back coffee for everybody. "You know how it's going to end," she said. "When he's picked up, he'll have her body in the trunk, or finally tell us where he left it. Oh, damn. I know these things happen, but—"

"She's a damn pretty girl," said Higgins gloomily. The sister had given them a photograph by now, bringing it in this morning, in case they wanted to send it around. She'd said miserably that she couldn't get in touch with Randy, Eileen's ex-boy friend, maybe he'd already gotten another girl. Eileen was as cute as a button, with a freckled tip-tilted nose, hair like a new penny, a wide friendly smiling mouth.

Into the little silence came Lake's voice from the corridor. "Yes, ma'am? What can we do for you?" Whatever reply he got was inaudible; in a minute he came down to the big office with a woman and said, "It's Mrs. Bussard, Lieutenant. About an I.D."

"Bussard?" said Mendoza. "I don't—"

Glasser got up and so did Wanda. "Yes, Mrs. Bussard?" They were surprised to see her, anybody, on that one. She looked as if life had used her hard; she was a woman looking to be too thin, with fast-graying brown hair, sagging lines in weather-beaten-looking skin; she was cheaply dressed in an ill-fitting navy pantsuit and white blouse.

"The police told me you'd found Gerald's body down here," she said in a flat voice. "The police in Bakersfield, I mean. I didn't even tell that officer I knew Gerald, but it got to bothering me. I was still married to him after all, I had a kind of duty. I suppose. To see he isn't buried in a—a potters' field or anything like that. I haven't got much money but I guess I could afford something. It got to bothering me, so I took off from work and drove down this morning."

"We're sorry to ask you." Glasser hesitated. "Isn't there anyone else who could—"

She shook her head. She looked very tired. "It's all right, I don't mind. Just looking at him. I just wondered—I guess Annie wasn't with him, then. What did he die of?"

"He shot himself, Mrs. Bussard," said Glasser quietly. That inquest was scheduled for tomorrow, along with one on Marion Cooper.

"Oh," she said. "Oh." She had taken the chair Mendoza pulled out for her. She leaned back in it and shut her eyes. After a long moment she said, "It's queer how things turn out. When we got married he'd just started his own business—nice roadside restaurant up there, good class. We were doing good for a while. But you wouldn't be interested in that, I'm sorry." She straightened up. "Where do I have to go?"

"Mrs. Bussard," said Wanda gently, "there was a girl with him. He'd shot her too. Would you know who she was? She was about twenty-three, a very pretty girl with long black hair and blue eyes."

She sagged in the chair. "Annie," she said. "Annie." Wanda fled down the hall for a glass of water; but she was sitting up straight again when she accepted it. She took a sip, and sat just holding the glass. They gave her time.

"So Annie's—gone too." She drew a shallow breath. "So I guess I got to tell about it. Annie—she was our daughter. Gerald's and mine. The youngest one. He—he did it to all of them—soon as they got to be thirteen, fourteen. You know what I mean. I never found out about Sandra, it just grieved me when she ran away. I don't know where she is, never heard. But after Julie run off she wrote me a letter, told me why—so I knew what was wrong with Annie. I was ashamed—tell anybody, have him put in jail—and then—then they just went away together, he took her away. That was five years back, I never heard nothing since." She put the glass down on Landers' desk and stood up. "I'd better go and look at them now," she said. "To say it is them, and whatever you want me to do."

Wanda and Glasser took her out.

There wasn't a smell of Rudy Bartovic all day. At five o'clock, after kicking it around with everybody in, Mendoza amended the A.P.B. to cover eight counties around. He could be anywhere.

Higgins went home early. Grace and Landers left about ten minutes later. Palliser was talking about dogs to Glasser, who didn't seem to be interested; he was saying that the obedience training Roberta had been doing with their German shepherd was really taking effect, it was a lot of work but with a dog like that worth it. Glasser was unresponsive. He hadn't written the final report on the Bussards yet. Palliser stabbed out a final cigarette and went out, and Glasser followed him. Wanda had already left.

Mendoza went back to his office for his hat, and when he came out, a messenger had just dropped off two manila folders. Lake said good night and left.

One was the autopsy report on Gregory Parmenter, the other, finally, the lab report on Marion Cooper's apartment. He took them back to his desk to glance at quickly. Parmenter: he'd been well beaten up, all right, but hadn't died of it directly; he'd had chronic heart disease, and the fatal attack had probably been brought on by the beating. Which was not much help, if interesting.

In the other report, there was just one detail which caught his eye. He reached for the phone book, looked at the clock, which told him it was five of six, reconsidered, and then said to himself, "*¿Por qué no?*"

If the man wasn't there, he could reach him tomorrow. But the man was there.

FIVE

Mendoza had called Hackett at home. He slid the Ferrari into the curb under the streetlight at five minutes to eight, and a couple of minutes later Hackett's Monte Carlo, its garish paint job not too visible in the dark, pulled up on the other side of the street. They both got out and met on the sidewalk.

"My God, Luis," said Hackett. In the unnatural sodium light of the arc lamp he looked a little sick. "What a thing."

"So. But once I'd heard that, as I told you, almost the foregone conclusion, ¿como no?"

They went up to the deep porch of the old-fashioned bungalow together, and Mendoza pushed the bell. After a minute Cooper opened the door. "Oh—you again," he said. "Hello. Have you—found out anything more?"

"I'm afraid so, Mr. Cooper," said Mendoza gently, and swept off his hat. "May we come in?"

They didn't say very much to the Coopers; there wasn't much to say, and the Coopers were silent and stunned, just staring dumbly at them.

"You understand, we'll have to talk to Harriet," said Mendoza.

Daniel Cooper looked at his mother. She said faintly, "She's—in her—I'll—" and went out like a sleepwalker.

She was an attractive child, not pretty-pretty, but characterful: the neat dark cap of hair, the clear hazel eyes, the small sober mouth. "Oh," she said, looking from Mendoza to Hackett, "you're the policemen."

"That's right, Harriet." Her grandmother eased her gently into a chair, and Mendoza sat down on the big ottoman opposite that. "You know we've been trying to find out what happened to your mother. We've been talking to people who knew her, and looking at that apartment. And we've just found out that she had a bottle of capsules of something called phenobarbital. Some of our men found the empty bottle in the wastepaper basket in the kitchen." She was listening politely, head down—or perhaps she wasn't listening. "There was a doctor's name on it, because it was a prescription. Dr. Adam Guilfoyle. I talked to him a couple of hours ago, and he told me some interesting things." She just sat there, unmoving. "You know what I'm talking about, don't you, Harriet? Your mother had an abscessed tooth a couple of months ago, and Dr. Guilfoyle gave her the prescription in case she had any pain after he'd taken the tooth out. But he told her to be careful. He knew your mother—she'd been a patient of his for six or seven years. And he told her to tell you to be careful. Because he knows you too, doesn't he? He takes care of your teeth too. And in fact, after your mother had gone to him then—in an emergency—you had an appointment with him, to be checked for any new cavities, just a couple of days later, didn't you? And Dr. Guilfoyle gave you a little lecture about those capsules he knew your mother had at home, didn't he? He knows that sometimes people your age are tempted to experiment with the pills, and he explained just how dangerous that could be."

She just sat there, very still. "You know you'll have to tell us about it," said Mendoza. "Or do you want us to guess?

You were the only one there, you see."

"Harriet, honey—" said Cooper chokingly.

She raised her eyes slowly and looked at him. "Do you—want me—to tell, Daddy?"

He could only nod silently. He got out, "You have to—be honest, honey."

Harriet said drearily, draggingly, "Well, all right. She didn't want me there or even like me much. It was just the money from Daddy she wanted. And she never cleaned the apartment, all the dishes were dirty all the time, all messy everywhere. And I didn't like that school. I just—I just want to live with Daddy and Grandma—they really want me. It got so I couldn't—hardly—stand it—I wanted so bad—to get away—but I never could because of the money from Daddy. And—that week—I was so ashamed—no clean clothes to put on, she forgot about the laundry, she was cross when I—I—I—all of a sudden I thought, if she just wasn't *there* anymore that would sort of fix everything. And I could stay with Daddy and Grandma all the time."

Cooper made a strangled sound. "So, tell us what you did that night," said Hackett.

She raised docile eyes. "I was thinking about it ever since I got home from school. She went out after dinner, she'd just brought a couple of hamburgers from McDonald's and mine was all cold and too red, I didn't eat much. And I knew she'd fix herself a drink before she went to bed, she always did lately. Lots of times I woke up when she came home. I'd hear her. And there wasn't much left in that bottle of scotch, I thought she'd prob'ly use it all. I remembered what Dr. Guilfoyle said. She hadn't used hardly any of those little capsules. So I took them all apart and put all the powder stuff into the bottle. And then I just went to bed. I heard her come in." Harriet was looking down at the floor again. "She was singing a song about blue skies, and she knocked over a chair in the kitchen."

Cooper put his hands over his face.

"Next morning I didn't—didn't look—it felt all funny, like

maybe I'd dreamed all that—but when I got home from school—I was scared, but I had—to look, and then I didn't know what to do, except just tell somebody." She looked squarely at Mendoza. "Are you—going to put me in jail for it?"

"We'll have to tell the story to a judge, Harriet," said Mendoza seriously, "and right now we'll have to take you to a place called Juvenile Hall, where you'll be staying until you see the judge." He flicked a glance at Hackett, who went to find the phone and call in.

Mrs. Cooper said in a thick voice, "She'll need—I'd better —a bag—" Harriet began to cry, slowly and tearlessly, and her grandmother went to her, led her out.

Cooper was standing with his back turned in front of the empty blackened hearth. "What—what's going to happen?" he asked in a dead tone.

"I don't know, Mr. Cooper. There'll be a hearing before a Juvenile Court judge. She's pretty young. But it wasn't exactly impulse, she'd planned it out—that'll be taken into consideration. They'll want a psychiatric evaluation, and pending the result of that—I can't tell you, but I'd rather doubt that she'll be held in custody. It's possible she'll just be put on probation and remanded to you—with a juvenile officer keeping a check on her behavior."

"Oh, God," said Cooper wearily, "I don't—know how to talk to her about it." He dragged a hand down over his face, and then he said suddenly, "It's my fault. Christ, it's all my fault. If I'd had the guts to fight Marion, insist on getting custody . . . God, I knew she was a bad mother. It was all my fault. My God, eleven—eleven years old—she didn't— really know what she was doing, did she?"

"Oh, yes, Mr. Cooper," said Mendoza steadily, "she knew. That's the worst of it. Just remember that."

A couple of policewomen from Juvenile Division came up to take Harriet in. Both she and her grandmother were crying then. Cooper hugged her, kissed her, told her they'd be coming to see her. Then he and his mother went into the house and shut the door.

Mendoza and Hackett went back to their cars without much exchange. There really wasn't much to say about Harriet.

On Thursday morning there were inquests scheduled for the Bussards, for Marion Cooper; Mendoza and Glasser would cover those, offer the formal testimony. There wasn't anything in on Bartovic at all. It was Higgins' day off.

Hackett and Palliser went back to the little quiet dead-end street to ask the neighbors if they knew of anybody who'd come to see Parmenter, about any relatives. After all, it was a settled neighborhood, and he'd lived there a long time.

Palliser went to try the places across the street. Hackett tried the neighbors immediately next to Parmenter.

Mrs. Klaber was a pleasant-faced, friendly middle-aged woman; her husband was at work, of course: he was a clerk at Bullocks' men's shop. "Well, she had a brother," she told Hackett doubtfully. "Mrs. Parmenter, I mean, she seemed to be a nice enough woman, what little I saw of her—but of course she died, it was cancer, and I couldn't tell you the man's name, not that he came to see them very often. Mr. Parmenter was a kind of recluse, nobody ever knew him very well."

At the house on the other side of Parmenter's, the rather attractive dark-haired Mrs. Hilbrand was on her knees weeding a flower bed at one side of the sparse front lawn, with a toddler about three riding a tricycle on the front walk. She recognized Hackett, asked him to sit down on the porch, accepted a cigarette, saying she was glad of an excuse to take a rest. "I don't remember anybody ever coming to see him— them. The wife was still alive when we bought this place, of course. They'd never had any children, and I guess there weren't any relatives. He was a sort of queer old man."

"We've gathered that," said Hackett.

"It was as if he didn't want any friends." The toddler

came staggering up the steps and solemnly showed Hackett a black-and-white stuffed dog.

"Nice doggie," he said. Hackett smiled at him and patted the dog obligingly. "Nice Pepper," crooned the toddler. "Pepper die and go to heaven."

"Yes, darling," she said gently, "but we're busy talking, you run and play. We're going to get a nice new doggie pretty soon. Mr. Parmenter was really an old grouch, to be plain about it. I was furious at him that time when Don fell down—it was last summer, a Sunday afternoon, and I was out with my sister. Oh, you don't know, of course, but Don—my husband—was in a terrible car accident last year, he lost a leg and the sight of one eye, and he was still getting used to the artificial leg. He fell in the back yard and couldn't get up, and Mr. Parmenter was out in his yard, Don called and asked for help and the old—well!—the old bustard just pretended he couldn't hear. You see what kind he was."

"I can think of other names," said Hackett sympathetically.

"It's just lucky, of course, that they held the job for Don— he's a desk clerk at the Ambassador, so the leg doesn't really bother him much. Haven't you found out anything about what happened to Mr. Parmenter?"

"Not very much," said Hackett.

"Well"—she gave him a friendly smile—"I suppose I'd better get back to the yard work."

He compared notes with Palliser, who had heard much the same thing from the other neighbors. "I don't," said Palliser, "see anywhere else to go on it."

Hackett agreed, rather bored with Gregory Parmenter. They drove out to Federico's, separately, for lunch, and met Mendoza and Glasser just going in. There hadn't yet been a smell of Bartovic, and Mendoza was feeling annoyed.

When they got back to the office, Lake said, "Business picking up some, Lieutenant. There was a new call ten minutes ago, body in MacArthur Park—Jase took it." And just then a light flashed on the switchboard and he plugged in automatically. "Robbery-Homicide, Sergeant Lake . . .

Oh. Oh? Yeah, he just came in. Palliser—it's Jase."

"Listen," said Grace, "I think you'd better come and look at this, John. You'll see what I mean when you get here."

Curious, Palliser went downstairs again and drove over to MacArthur Park. There are a few privileges granted to police officers, and one of them is parking in red-painted curb zones; parking slots were always rare along here, but he left the car in front of an office building across Wilshire and walked over into the park. Just up by the little lake on this side were Grace, a uniformed man, and two women; beyond them a man slumped on a park bench. They were the only people in the park. It was rather queer, thought Palliser, remembering Eileen, that people didn't seem to go and sit in parks anymore, feeding the pigeons and enjoying the sunshine; maybe these hectic days they just didn't have time. And MacArthur was a nice city park, too, with its war memorial and green lawns, and little lake, and the clean new bright skyline of all the high-rise buildings along Wilshire, bisecting it.

He came up to Grace, who was brushing his hairline mustache back and forth as a sign of irritation, and said, "What's up?"

"This is Sergeant Palliser," said Grace. "Mrs. Stubbs and Mrs. Ryder. Suppose you tell him the story over again, Mrs. Stubbs."

"Why, all right." She was quite willing to talk. They were both nondescript commonplace females, middle-aged, a little dowdy; this one had brown hair fast turning gray and a round face and tortoiseshell glasses, the other one was thinner with sandy hair. "It was awful, just awful. We were just coming along here, to get the bus up on Sixth, easier to cut across the park. We both live up on San Marino, we're neighbors, and there wasn't a soul here except the man on the bench. And we were talking, not paying much attention to him, but when we were about right where we are now this young fellow went up to him and said something, I don't know what, and then, I couldn't believe my eyes, right here in the open in broad daylight, he took a knife out of his pocket and stabbed

103

him! Just stabbed him two or three times, and Edith sort of screamed and I guess I did too, and then he came running right past us, he didn't take any notice of us at all—most terrible thing I ever saw—and we went to look and the poor man was dead! All that blood—"

"Go and take a look, John," said Grace. "There's a lab unit on the way to take pictures."

The uniformed man was brooding over the lone figure on the bench up there beside the lake. Palliser took a look and uttered a few swearwords. He went back to Grace.

". . . Civic duty," said Mrs. Ryder as he came up, "of course we'll be glad to give you statements about it. But as to identifying anybody, well, it was just a flash, and we were both so startled—I couldn't say I'd know him again—young, and he had light hair—"

"He was tall—"

"Not as tall as you," said Mrs. Ryder, looking at Palliser.

"I'd say about as tall. He had on a white shirt—"

"Light blue."

"I'm sure, Edith—"

"So am I. And he could change his shirt, I suppose."

Grace had their addresses; they finally went on their way, the lab unit arrived, and Palliser and Grace went back to the body. "And by God," said Palliser, "this is just too long a coincidence, Jase! Look at him—just look—in a general way, he's a ringer for Joe Kelly—and, by God, even that old wino on the Row! A superficial resemblance, but the same type. They were all in the sixties, middle-sized, ordinary-looking —all knifed—and I don't buy the coincidence. And Kelly said the fellow who followed him was young and had light hair— What the hell is this?"

"I thought you'd be interested," said Grace.

"And who the hell is this one?" It was a while before they could look; the lab men were always thorough. Eventually Marx handed over a billfold. It contained seven dollars and fifty-three cents, various credit cards, a membership card for a local Elks club, and identification for Robert Barker, an address on Park View Street two blocks away.

They walked up there; it was a neat little old duplex. The woman who answered the door was comfortably round and pink-faced and smiling, gray-haired, her hands floury. "I'm sorry, I was in the middle of mixing up biscuits, what is it? What kind of a thing is that?" She stared at Palliser's badge.

There weren't any right ways to break bad news. She said at first, blankly, "Why, yes, Robert's up at the park, he's just getting over the flu, hasn't gone back to work yet, he thought the sun would be good for—" And then after silence she said, "But Robert can't be *dead!* How could Robert be dead?"

The woman who lived on the other side of the duplex, a widow named McNally, came over on appeal, saying she'd known the Barkers for years, was a good friend. "Oh, Nellie!" sobbed Mrs. Barker. "Oh, Nellie—got to call Rita and Bob Junior—I don't understand it—he was feeling so much better this morning—"

"You leave everything to me, Dottie." She could, of course, tell them this and that more sensibly.

"Coincidence I do not buy," said Palliser angrily, back at the office. "And I thought I was woolgathering, saying there was a vague resemblance between the old wino and Kelly, but now look at this!"

Mendoza was interested. "Yes, it's a pattern, but for God's sake what kind?"

"How the hell can anybody guess? But look at it! They all conform generally to the same description. On the wino, anybody down there might knife anybody for the price of a bottle of muscatel, but for what it's worth he had a buck or two on him. Kelly, the inoffensive ordinary retired railroader. No enemies, no money, no reason for anybody to kill him. And now here's Robert Barker, the same damn kind. He worked for Greyhound, ticket seller at the Sixth Street station, a year off retirement. Quiet family man, little money, no enemies. He wasn't robbed—he had seven dollars on him."

"Mmh, yes," said Mendoza. "A pattern. But it doesn't point in any direction. I suppose there wasn't any connection between them?"

"Hell," said Palliser thoughtfully, "I wonder if there could have been? That is a thought. Between Kelly and Barker, it's possible. They lived in the same general area, had the same sort of backgrounds. I'll have a look. But for God's sake, it's senseless—knifing a man in the open, with witnesses—"

"Who don't sound like such reliable witnesses," said Mendoza dryly, and Grace laughed ruefully.

"How many ever are?"

And just then Sergeant Lake came trotting down the hall. "We've got Bartovic! They just picked him up down in Santa Monica."

The squad car from Santa Monica delivered Rudy Bartovic to the central jail twenty minutes later, and Mendoza, Hackett, Palliser and Grace were waiting for him. His car, the old T-bird, was being towed in for lab examination.

They started in to grill him then and there. Unless they found some good solid evidence in his car, or broke him down to confess that he'd attacked and abducted Eileen Mooney, they couldn't hold him more than twenty-four hours without a warrant. And he was a punk; he might be prone to violence, he might be a user, but he didn't have a long or bad record, he wasn't a real tough, and he might come apart right away.

He wasn't an attractive specimen, slouching at the little table in the interrogation room. He was a big hulk, long unkempt dark hair, beetling eyebrows, a strong prow of a nose. He wasn't long on brains, and he was naturally suspicious of police.

"All right, Rudy, where's Eileen?" Higgins began it, grim and professional, looming over him.

"What the hell you mean? I don't know why you picked me up, I haven't done anything."

"Eileen Mooney. Where is she? Where'd you take her?"

"I didn't take her anywhere. What the hell?"

"You know what we're talking about. What did you do to her?"

"I don't know what the hell you're talkin' about. The last time I saw Eileen was last Friday night."

"And you gave her a rough time, didn't you, Rudy?" Mendoza cut in coldly. "You thought she'd be an easy girl, you were mad when she fought you, weren't you? Maybe you'd been thinking about that, wanted to get even. How about it, Rudy?"

"I—she hadn't no call to do that, I never meant any harm. I don't know what you mean."

"Where is she, Rudy?"

"I don't know!" he snarled.

"Come on, come on," said Higgins roughly, "we can read it plain enough, Rudy. You saw her pass on her way to the park, you followed her and saw her sitting there—nobody else around. You probably drove your car down to a handy spot alongside the park—and you grabbed her there, and she fought you again, didn't she?"

"What did you do to her to make her bleed that much, Rudy?" asked Grace.

"I never did nothing to her."

"Then where is she?" Mendoza's voice cut like a knife. "It's pretty damn obvious she was taken away from the park by force, and you were the one right there on the spot—you were the one who'd been pestering her for dates, took her out last week and damn near raped her, and got mad at her when she resisted—"

"I don't know what the hell you're all talkin' about. I don't know nothing about Eileen."

"Where've you been since last Tuesday?" asked Higgins abruptly.

"Oh, for God's sake. Around. I been feeling lousy, no job, everything gone to hell, Ma nag at me—I just didn't feel like goin' home. I drove around—I—Tuesday? You got me confused—I went to a couple movies somewhere, and then—since then—I been with a girl friend down in Santa Monica, that's were I got picked up."

"What's her name?"

"Doreen. Doreen Segura. Twenty-fourth Street."

They went all around it again and again, and he kept saying the same things. It was after six-thirty when Mendoza said, "Damn it, leave it overnight. We can hold him until tomorrow afternoon. See what the lab turns on the car." And those boys were finicky and thorough: it would take time to vacuum that heap and examine everything under the microscope; but some blood, a few of Eileen's copper-penny hairs in a suggestive place, when he knew the evidence was there he might change his tune. See what the girl said. "And leave a note for the night watch, as soon as they've chased her down, call me on it *immediatamente!*"

At ten-thirty when the phone rang Mendoza was dealing himself crooked poker hands on the coffee table in the living room. Alison was upstairs doing her nails, and the cats had gone to visit Mairí's little downstairs suite, being fascinated with her knitting.

"Yes?"

"Join the force and see life," said Conway. "This Segura female is a topless dancer at a third-rate club down here. I don't know how honest she is, but, Christmas, chief, she is stacked. I've been talking to her backstage. She says she hadn't laid eyes on Bartovic in about six months until he landed at her place around noon on Wednesday. She felt sorry for him, down on his luck, and let him stay. He'd been there ever since—well, she was out working last night—working, hah—but he was there when she got home at four A.M."

"*¡Condenación!* That's no damn use to us—he could have killed the girl Tuesday morning and dropped the body somewhere by Tuesday afternoon."

"Yeah, I know, but that's what she says. She also says he had some pretty good grass on him. If he'd been high on the pot, he might be a little vague about times."

"And if he'd been smoking pot he might have been sniffing coke or hitting the angel dust, which would make it all the likelier he'd do a murder," said Mendoza irritably.

"Something might show up in the car," said Conway.

Mendoza was annoyed. He put the phone down and unprecedentedly went out to the kitchen to get himself a drink. El Señor, who could hear that particular cupboard door open the length of the house away, appeared as if by magic on the countertop and demanded his share. "Ought to join A.A.," muttered Mendoza at him. "This is not good for cats. You had your daily ration before dinner, *borrachón!*"

Before Conway got back, Schenke and Piggott were called out to another heist, at a bar on Second. There were only four witnesses. "It's been a slow night," said the bartender, whose name was O'Toole. "I was going to close early, just these three guys here, and then he walked in." They all gave the same description: blond, big, husky, with a big gun. "And when he says, hand it over and do it quick, I guess I was a little shook —it was so sudden—and he got real ugly and says, I said move it, man, and damned if he didn't shoot at me—I felt the damn bullet go past. Oh, and he had a real broad southern accent." They all confirmed that.

"Well, well," said Schenke. "Our hair-trigger artist again, by all that. Where'd the slug hit?" He spotted the hole in the wall over the bar, got out his knife and prodded for it, got it out looking fairly intact.

They all offered to come in and look at mug shots, but that would probably be a waste of time. And he hadn't gotten much; the customers figured out that they'd lost about fifteen dollars all told, and he'd only gotten thirty from the register.

Writing the report on that took them to the end of the shift. Piggott drove home through the largely empty dark streets, the traffic lights uncannily dark too. He was tired; maybe he was getting spring fever. At the apartment, he climbed the stairs quietly, fumbled with his key and went into the living room. He stood there for a few minutes watching the big lighted aquarium in one corner, with the beautiful tropical fish gliding around it smooth and lazy. He felt himself relaxing just for the sight; and tomorrow was his day off. He undressed in the dark and got into bed beside Prudence, and she stirred and said drowsily, "Matt," before going to sleep again.

On Friday morning Higgins looked at Piggott's report and said, "So I was dragging my heels on it. The hair-trigger's not a local. Definitely the southern accent. So let's ask NCIC if they've got anybody similar listed." He went down to Communications to send off a query.

Mendoza was already on the phone to SID, but it was an hour before Duke and Fisher came into the office. They looked glum and tired; Duke kept rubbing his eyes. "I know you've had the hell of a job at short notice," said Mendoza. "But we can't hold him past four P.M.—"

"I don't think you can hold him at all," said Duke. "We've got a few suggestive little things but not really enough."

"Damnation. What have you got?"

The two SID men had been up all night going over Bartovic's car. Wanda brought in coffee; everybody was there, waiting to hear what they had. "There was some blood on the spare tire in the trunk," said Duke. "Not much, just some. Three red-blond hairs on the front seat, and a nearly new lipstick that looks like a color a redhead might use. Also a female handkerchief, pretty clean, with the initial *E* on it, also in the front seat."

"*¡Diez millón demonios!*" said Mendoza. "She could have lost those in the car on Friday night. Which Bartovic would realize."

"There was the dust from marijuana leaves all over the place," said Fisher. "The car's been at the beach a lot, beach sand all over too. More hairs, probably female, in the back seat—black and brown. That's really about it."

"What type was the blood?" asked Mendoza.

110

"O." Fisher didn't comment, and Mendoza snarled. That was the commonest type; also Eileen Mooney's type. But it wasn't enough.

"If we ask him about it," said Higgins, "he'll say he scraped his knuckles changing a tire."

They made another try at it, of course. Mendoza, Hackett and Higgins went over to the jail and spent a while grilling Bartovic again, going at him hot and heavy. He just kept saying he didn't know nothing about Eileen, he hadn't seen her since last week, he didn't know what the hell they were talking about.

"We can't hold him," said Mendoza with a vicious snap of his lighter, on the jail steps. "Minus a body, it's nothing." They were all annoyed about it, but it couldn't be helped. And even in the great urban sprawl of L.A., there were places a body could lie for months without being found.

They stopped for lunch, and got back to the office just after one. The kickback from NCIC had come in. Known and currently wanted violent heisters from below the Mason-Dixon line, or possessing southern accents wherever they had latest violated the law, and corresponding to the descriptions, numbered exactly three, on two jobs. A pair of brothers from Tennessee, Walt and Gilbert Craven. And Leroy Rogers, wanted on a job in Georgia. The Cravens were wanted for a heist in Nashville where a man had been shot and seriously wounded. Rogers was wanted for a homicide pulled on the Georgia heist. All of them matched the description, of course.

"Well," said Higgins, looking at that, "let's see what these lawmen might know about these characters, if any of them have any relatives or pals out here. Of course, they might have landed here by accident, that kind just does what comes naturally." But leads turned up in odd places sometimes, and it was usually the dogged routine that broke cases. He glanced at the clock. "Time differences—oh, the day shift'll still be on back there." He sat down at his desk and picked up the phone.

Palliser and Grace came in, heard the news about Bartovic

and cussed. They looked tired and annoyed. Palliser said to Wanda, "We could both use some coffee."

"Wait on you just because I'm female," she grumbled, but she went to get it.

"Well," said Palliser, "we now know there was no connection between Kelly and Barker. Both Simms and Moreno are definite on that. Certainly neither of them could have had any connection with the derelict."

"The autopsy report on Kelly came in while you were gone," said Wanda brightly.

"So," said Mendoza, "let's see if it has anything to tell us." He took it from her, scanned it rapidly, shrugged and passed it over to Palliser. "*Nada absolutamente.* Healthy specimen for his age, slightly enlarged heart. Approximate time of death . . . And the knife tapers from an inch and a half to a quarter inch, and has a serrated edge. Even if the autopsy on Barker says that too, that's an ordinary-sized knife, you can buy one in any hardware store."

"Well, there's just one thing struck me," said Grace. He stretched out his legs, leaning back and sipping coffee.

"Any idea is welcome," said Palliser.

"That bum on the Row," said Grace, and his brown face wore a meditative expression. "Over there, you could knife a man on the street and never be noticed, so many of the crowd being drunks and dopies. But on Kelly, you know, he used a little rudimentary cunning, lying in wait for him like that. And then on Barker he did it right out in the open, in a fairly decent area of town, middle of the day in front of two witnesses, no caution at all. It looks to me as if he's a nut, and getting nuttier fast."

"Thank you," said Palliser. "That hadn't occurred to me, Jase. So it could be the next time he hits, it'll be in the middle of a crowd and somebody might nab him."

"Lieutenant," said Lake down the hall, "the D.A.'s office wants to talk to you."

"Oh, hell," said Mendoza. It was, of course, one of the deputy D.A.'s wanting to talk about Harriet Cooper. He swiveled around in his desk chair so he would have a nice view, and lit a cigarette, and disposed himself to listen.

Higgins got some information from the southern lawmen, but not much. Rogers was from Texas originally. It wasn't known whether any of them had relations in California, but it was possible they may have some pals here: they had all spent time in federal prisons. The helpful lawmen said they'd do some phoning and asking around, and get back to L.A. with anything they picked up. And about that time, which was three-thirty, a new call came in and the address was Wesley Avenue so Grace went out with him on it. That was a solid black area down there.

The patrolman from the squad was black too, a rookie by the name of Turner, and he was somewhat helplessly trying to comfort the brown young woman sitting on the front porch sobbing. It was a short street of modest old houses, for the most part neatly kept up; this one was a small white frame place with a minute strip of lawn in front.

"She was just starting to tell me about it when she broke down," said Turner. "I guess she's got reason—she said that's her mother in there. Dead some time, I'd say." He swallowed; as a rookie he hadn't yet seen many dead bodies. "Look, miss —I'm sorry, but the detectives'll have to have some information."

She tried to control herself; she choked back the sobs and wiped her eyes. She was a nice-looking young woman in rather smart clothes. "I know—try," she gulped. "Mother— Mrs. Edna Patterson—we've been away—and—her old f-friend called to say she wasn't—at Wednesday prayer meeting—Mrs. Altura Fielding—and was she sick, because she c-c-couldn't get her on the phone—and I—c-couldn't either so I—came—"

There weren't any neighbors out on either side, but it was a working-class neighborhood and there might be nobody at home.

"Can we hear your name?" said Grace in his soft voice.

She peered at him over the wadded-up handkerchief. "I'm —Linda Gilman. Mrs. I'm sorry, I tried to keep my head, called the police, and then—seeing her l-like that—and the house— Oh, I've got to call Dave, I've got to call Dave—"

"Have you got a car, Mrs. Gilman?" There wasn't one parked on the street nearby.

"C-came on the bus—"

"Well, now, if you'll just wait a few minutes and answer a few questions, we'll have Patrolman Turner here drive you home, and you can get hold of your husband. Is that all right?"

She gulped and nodded. "But it's not—it's not—only Mother! That's bad enough—it's terrible, it's terrible—but where are all her things? All the furniture—we were all b-brought up here, it's home—thirty years—and all the things we saved up for, nice things—and the last thing Dad made her, that cedar chest in her room—mantel clock—the platform rocker Dad always—"

Grace patted her shoulder. "You wait just a couple of minutes."

The front door was open. They went in, and looked. The house was larger than it seemed from outside; there were three bedrooms, a separate dining area off the kitchen. From the kitchen window was a view of a pleasant back yard.

The body of the woman was in the largest bedroom. She was a chocolate-brown woman probably around sixty, small and thin, and she was wearing a pink nightgown and a blue corduroy bathrobe. It looked as if she'd been strangled, and as Turner said, she'd been dead for some time.

And the house was empty. There wasn't any furniture in it at all, any carpets, even any pictures on the walls. They couldn't open drawers or cupboards until the lab had been through here, but those might be empty too.

The only thing left in the whole house except the telephone was in the middle of the kitchen floor: a pair of scuffed, worn tapestry bedroom slippers.

"My sweet Christ," said Grace, awed.

"We'd better get the lab on it quick," said Higgins stolidly, turning away.

It was a funny thing, he'd been a cop for over twenty years, and a detective for fourteen, and in that time he'd seen a lot of bloody messes and human misery and sordid little tragedies and irrational suffering. But, ridiculously, he felt tears burn his eyes, and he knew it would be a while before he forgot that—two limp, worn, comfortable bedroom slippers in the middle of a kitchen floor. Marking a place where home had become unsafe, and a humdrum life, death.

Hackett walked into Mendoza's office at nine o'clock on Saturday morning and found him sitting with his eyes shut and the County Guide open on his desk. "Are you practicing going into trance or what? I always said you ought to try a crystal ball."

Mendoza opened his eyes, sat up and got out a cigarette. "*Mas vale tarde que nunca.* Better late than never. Like the lost horse and the idiot boy, I was just trying to think where I might have dropped off Eileen's body if I was Rudy Bartovic."

"You come to any conclusion?"

"Maybe," said Mendoza. "He finished with Eileen—whatever he did to her, and we can guess—and he left her in the trunk of the car, wrapped in a blanket or something, while he went to that porno movie house—I'll lay a bet it was porn. Sometime that night he could have been down at the beach— he landed at Doreen's place that next noon. It's just possible, Arturo, that he dropped her off the end of the pier."

Hackett nodded slowly. "I can see it. If so, she'll turn up soon. Tides—and it's nice weather, a lot of people flocking to the beaches."

"I don't know anything about tides. I just think I'll call Harbor—and the Santa Monica boys—and ask to be told about any new bodies they come across."

"Damn it, there should have been evidence in his car."

"*Paciencia*. Even the smart lab boys can't pick it up where it isn't."

Sergeant Farrell looked in. "Oh, there you are. Call for you, Art."

Hackett went back to his desk, and picked up the phone. "Sergeant Hackett."

"Oh," said a bright female voice, "I didn't—Well, the manageress said it was someone asking about Alice and I should call this number. I'm Angela Bickerstaff, and Alice—"

"Oh, yes, Mrs. Bickerstaff. Is Miss McLennan at home yet?"

"Oh, no. I didn't quite understand—"

"Well, I'd like to talk to you, if I could see you now?"

"I suppose so," she said, sounding bewildered.

And he didn't know what he was wasting the time for, but he drove over to Baxter Avenue and found Mrs. Bickerstaff in the apartment across the hall from Alice McLennan's. She was a little brown bird of a woman, possibly fifty, with a kitten face, bright brown eyes. She looked at the badge and said, "My goodness, police. What's it about? It isn't—is Alice all right?"

"Quite all right as far as I know. We're rather anxious to talk to her," explained Hackett. "It's about her former employer, Mr. Parmenter. He's just, well, died, and the circumstances—"

"Oh," she said. "He has? Isn't that strange, and Alice'll be *very* interested. I wonder—" but she didn't say what.

"I understand you and Miss McLennan are quite good friends. I just wondered if you knew why she quit her job with Mr. Parmenter. She'd worked for him quite a while, hadn't she?"

"Four years," said Mrs. Bickerstaff promptly. "It didn't pay much, but she has a little family money from a trust too. I don't know, Mr. Hackett, but we probably will when Alice comes back. She was very upset about it, about quitting her job. That was on March nineteenth, and I didn't happen to see her until the next Monday, the twenty-first, and I knew she was upset and worried about something. But Alice is pretty closemouthed, she's one to sort of mull things over until she makes up her mind about something. All she said to me then was that she had a good reason to quit the job. And you see, I'd been worried because the baby was sick, my daughter's baby, little Sue—and it was that next Saturday, Lisa—my daughter—called to ask could I come and help. So I packed a bag, it was about ten in the morning, and when I left I went across the hall to tell Alice where I'd be—and she was just coming out her door with a suitcase. And Mickey."

"Yes," said Hackett patiently.

"Well, she said she was going up to Big Bear or somewhere, she just felt she needed to get away for a while. I think she'd have told me more about it if we hadn't both been in a hurry, you see how it was, she said she'd been going to tape a note on my door, tell me where she'd gone. And she said"—Mrs. Bickerstaff cocked her brown head at him—"she'd tell me all about it when she got back, she couldn't bear to talk about it now, but she said the reason she'd quit her job, she'd found out something about Mr. Parmenter that was so terrible it just didn't bear thinking about, and he was the wickedest man in the world. And she grabbed up Mickey's leash and started downstairs."

Hackett stared at her. "Now what in—"

"Well, it was funny," she said thoughtfully. "I suppose we'll find out when Alice comes back. At least, thank goodness, the baby's fine now."

SIX

~~~~~~~~~~~~~~~~~~~~~~~~~~~~~~

Grace and Higgins were down on Wesley Street talking to neighbors of Edna Patterson's. The lab men had done some work here yesterday, and were back again today, now busy dusting the whole place for possible prints.

The neighbors on one side were Albert and Maria Jimson, and they were ordinary honest people; he drove a truck for a laundry, and they were both in their forties, with children grown and away. They were shocked and grieved about Mrs. Patterson, a fine woman, they said. Neighborly, and it was a nice family, two sons and a daughter, all doing well. Mrs. Jimson worked too, selling on commission for a local furniture store, and neither of them had seen Mrs. Patterson since Monday when she'd been putting her refuse can out as usual for the weekly pickup on Tuesday morning. They hadn't heard any disturbance, any night; and they'd been home Monday and Tuesday nights, watching TV until around eleven.

It looked as if she had been killed either Monday or Tuesday, but then what the people on the other side had to say changed that—which they'd eventually have seen for themselves. Mr. and Mrs. Fred Leaman, who hadn't seen her to speak to since Sunday, when they saw her leaving for church, had noticed that her refuse can, emptied, had been taken back to the garage sometime on Tuesday. That, of course, left Tuesday night still, but narrowed the time a little. They were another upright pair of citizens: he worked for the Parks and Recreation Department. None of them had heard any unusual sounds from Mrs. Patterson's house, noticed anyone going in there. The Leamans had been out on Tuesday night, visiting friends, but home on Monday. Watching TV.

Grace met Higgins briefly in mid block, and Higgins hadn't heard anything helpful either. "Just what a nice woman she was. What a nice family. The husband died of a heart attack last year, only sixty-three, he worked for a construction company. She probably didn't have much—his little pension, and she'd just applied for Social Security, and probably the children helped her out. Nobody heard or saw anything, and both nights most people were home, watching TV."

"I'm beginning to think," said Grace, "that TV is the curse of the twentieth century." They split up again; he crossed the street. And of course you got a cross section of people in any big-city neighborhood, people of all sorts, but after the upstanding respectability of the Jimsons and Leamans, the house directly across the street provided a violent contrast. The door was opened by a gangling, very black fellow in dirty jeans and a torn sweat shirt, smelling of beer and sweat; in the living room behind him a TV was blaring sports news. Somewhere a baby yelled. He told Grace they didn't pay any notice to neighbors, and was annoyed when Grace insisted on seeing his wife. She was a superficially pretty slattern, with a yelling baby on one shoulder. She said eagerly, "Did she really get murdered? Honest to God! She was an old bitch, so damn uppity and look down her nose, goin' to church alla time." They hadn't seen or heard a thing.

Next door to that place he found the Wisters, a young couple in a nice clean neat house, who couldn't tell him anything. Wister was a waiter at a very top class restaurant in Beverly Hills, and didn't get home until midnight. Mrs. Wister and her mother had been making new curtains for the kitchen and bedroom every night this week; they hadn't seen or heard anything out of the ordinary. They were shocked and frightened by the murder; Wister said, "The crime rate's just awful. This is a pretty quiet neighborhood, but I guess it can happen anywhere."

Nobody, of those who had been at home those two nights, had heard or seen anything unusual; and most of the people seemed to be honest citizens. "Damn it, Jase," said Higgins, looking up and down the shabby little street, "that must have been a hell of a lot of time and work, to clean out the whole house. When we moved, it took five men half a day to get everything loaded."

"Yes, and that's another thing," said Grace.

They'd come down in Higgins' Pontiac; they abandoned the unhelpful neighbors and drove up to Hollywood, to the Gilmans' apartment.

Linda Gilman's husband was there; he owned his own printing shop; and her two brothers, both older, settled family men. Roland Patterson was a dental technician, Ben Patterson manager of a Safeway supermarket. They had been trying to draw up a list of the contents of the house. Higgins and Grace looked at it, and Grace said, "Nobody moved all that in a single night alone. There must have been at least four or five men." There had been three double beds, the refrigerator, gas stove, washer and dryer, kitchen table and chairs, a big couch, four upholstered chairs from the living room, mirrors—they knew now, the only things left in the house were her clothes in the closet, linens, dishes in the kitchen. They wouldn't have gotten anything for those.

"Was this all pretty good stuff?" Higgins asked Linda.

"Well, yes, it is. Not the most expensive, but we always got the best we could afford, and all of this she'd had for years."

"And these days the solid good old stuff goes for quite a price at the secondhand stores," said Higgins. "It could have amounted to quite a nice piece of loot."

He expanded on that to Grace over lunch, and Grace said, "Granted. But just think about it a minute. Records can give us the names and pedigrees of a hundred burglars. But they're usually shy birds. Would types like that commit a murder for a houseful of furniture?"

"Well, when you put it like that—" said Higgins. "I see what you mean."

Mendoza stared at Hackett. "*¡Parece mentira!* The wickedest man in the world! Now that's very interesting, Art. I do wonder what she'd found out about him."

"I'll tell you one little notion that occurred to me," said Hackett. "She might have felt like that about Parmenter if she'd found out he'd been peddling the pills to the neighborhood kids. Or even, possibly, supplying a pusher."

"Oh, yes, that I can see. You know, your old recluse without any friends begins to interest me, *amigo*. Let's go and ask questions around that block."

"I've done some of that, and nobody really knew him."

"Maybe you didn't ask the right questions."

They drove over to the tired old block of businesses on Alvarado, and talked to the other business people. It wasn't a block to attract much foot traffic, only a little way above the Hollywood freeway, residential streets not so immediately joining it; a block or two away, the looming bulk of the old Queen of the Angels hospital.

The young man in the music store, behind his beard, was uninterested. It was a part-time job for him and he didn't know any of the people along here. The two maiden sisters who kept the doughnut shop had thought Mr. Parmenter was a little queer. Unfriendly. Children, or teen-agers, frequenting the pharmacy? They couldn't say they'd specially noticed many going in and out. There weren't many around here as a rule. The languid woman at the dress shop tried mildly to flirt with Mendoza, and didn't know a thing about the pharmacy or Mr. Parmenter.

At the cleaning shop next door to the pharmacy they met

Mr. Benjamin Rauschman, who tried to pump them for details of Parmenter's death. "He was a queer one all right," he said, unrepentant when Hackett squelched him with the routine platitude of police policy. And at Mendoza's question about kids, teen-agers, he leaped to the conclusion, eager and helpful. "You're thinking he was maybe selling the pills on the side to the kids? I wouldn't know about that." Mr. Rauschman was short and squat, with beautiful dark curling hair, alive dark eyes in a narrow face. "I didn't know the man—he was always polite enough, good morning, nice day, that was as far as it went—but I got the impression he was honest enough. Wasn't he?"

"I'll tell you, Mr. Rauschman," said Mendoza, "we don't know much about him either."

"Is that so?" said Rauschman. He accepted the offered cigarette and let Mendoza light it. "Well, I'll tell you something that probably doesn't mean one damn thing, but it struck me as—funny. Just funny." They waited, and he looked at the cigarette. "It just so happens that we got a married daughter lives up in Hollywood, and she's expecting a baby, and she hasn't been so good. Has to keep lying down a lot. So a good many nights, the last four or five months, the wife and I've been going up there so the wife can help out in the house and so on. And living over on Montana, naturally I take Sunset and go right past this corner, see? Well, old Parmenter, he always closed the store at six and went home. Same as all the rest of us along here, nothing open at night. But I tell you, three out of five nights we go past here, seven, seven-thirty, the pharmacy was lit up. He was there, or somebody was."

"What?" said Hackett. "I'll be damned."

"Maybe he was working on his books, or his income tax," said Rauschman, shrugging. "I wouldn't know."

Mendoza was rocking back and forth, heel to toe. "That's very interesting," he said gently. "I think I'd like a look at that place, Art—have you got the keys?" Rauschman watched them out with lively curiosity in his bright dark eyes.

"There's nothing here," said Hackett, unlocking the door

of the Independent Pharmacy. "We've pawed all over everything. And it's all just what you'd expect, just his account books, receipts, ordinary stock. And I wonder what the hell will happen to it, whatever he's got in the bank, the house, when there aren't any relatives. I suppose the state will come in for it."

Mendoza was prowling around, looking at everything. He said, "It doesn't look like a very prosperous business. I'd say he was just about making a living. Why did he need a clerk? He couldn't have been too busy to wait on all the trade himself."

"I suppose he wanted a woman who knew the cosmetic stock and so on."

"*¿Como?*" Mendoza penetrated back to the big storeroom behind the body of the shop. It was largely bare, shelves at one side holding extra stock of miscellaneous items. There was a large folding table against the back wall, stacked folding chairs. There was a container for holding the delivered spring water, and the bottle was half empty.

"There's nothing in the lab report either," said Hackett. "I finally got it yesterday, and as I said, I don't think whoever killed him went into the house at all. The lab dusted every surface they could reach and by all the latents there hadn't been anybody but him in the house for years, except the Coffman woman, and she kicked up a hell of a fuss at having her prints taken for comparison. I just can't imagine what was behind it. He could easily have made an enemy, the queer old cuss he was, but nothing says who."

"Yes," said Mendoza. "But why the hell should he come back here at night? It's not as if he—mmh—had to hide the pornography from a loving wife and family, and it'd be easier and safer to get drunk at home if he was a secret drinker—"

"He wasn't. Liquor costs too much."

"Well, you're right, there's nothing here. And SID is usually thorough, but I think I'd like a look at the house."

"Oh, for God's sake, if you want to waste the time . . ."

They went over to the quiet little backwater and parked in

front of the old frame house. Hackett unlocked the front door and they went in. It was a gloomy dank place, the few bare sticks of furniture, the stained walls, the uncarpeted floors redolent not so much of asceticism as of meanness. Mendoza went around opening cupboards and drawers and looking in closets, and Hackett asked, "What are you looking for?"

"I haven't the faintest idea," said Mendoza. "But I do wonder, Art, how he spent his evenings? He couldn't work in his garden after dark. There isn't a book or a magazine here, or a TV set, or a radio. Why the hell *did* he go back to the store at night? There's nothing like that there either."

Hackett trailed him patiently. "Your invisible crystal ball telling you something, *compadre*?"

"Just following my nose." Mendoza wound up out in the garage, which didn't have a workbench; there was just the old Ford sitting there, and everything was dusty and dirty. Mendoza came out, automatically brushing at his silver-gray Dacron suit.

"He was," said Hackett, "a professional blackmailer. Somewhere here there's a stash of incriminating information on some millionaires?"

"I wonder," said Mendoza seriously. "What about his banking records?"

"All perfectly straightforward. We found his bankbooks. You're right, he wasn't making any fat profit."

"What the hell was he doing," said Mendoza, "that he had to go back there at night?" He opened the door and went into the house again, into the old-fashioned square service porch. Hackett followed him. Mendoza stood gazing around meditatively, and then raised his eyes to the ceiling. "Well, now, I wonder," he said. "Do you remember that corpse we found under the trapdoor in that apartment?"

"That you found," said Hackett. "Vividly. You may remember that that was how I met my wife."

"Yes," said Mendoza. "A very ingenious hiding place if it had worked. I saw a ladder somewhere, go and get it, will you?"

The ladder was, in fact, leaning against the wall just outside the back door; Hackett brought it in and set it up. The
little trapdoor in the ceiling was intended as access for elec-
tricians and plumbers, to the wires and pipes above the ceiling; it was about two feet by three. Mendoza mounted the
ladder and pushed at it. It was just resting on a frame, and
moved obligingly aside. Mendoza went up another step and
shoved one arm inside.

"Let me guess," said Hackett. "Mice."

"¡Anda!" said Mendoza. "Something. But what?" He
reached in both arms, and brought out a stack of paper; the
ladder rocked on the uneven floor, Hackett grabbed it, and a
shower of leaflets and pamphlets fluttered down, with a couple of heavier books.

"What the hell—"

Mendoza came down and dived for a handful. He looked
at it and said, "¡Qué interesante es! So that's what Mr. Parmenter was up to. Now we know."

All of the crudely printed leaflets emanated from something called the Brotherhood of the Superior Race. Hackett
looked through the one Mendoza handed him. "One of these
white-supremacy outfits? I'll be damned—"

"A little more wholesale," said Mendoza, scanning the
thicker pamphlet he'd just picked up.

The Brotherhood of the Superior Race, by the contents of
all this printed material, didn't like anybody very much except themselves. They had no use at all for Jews, Catholics,
Negroes, Orientals, foreigners of any kind or presumably any
possible visitors from outer space. There were stacks and
stacks of the stuff up there, and some privately printed books,
all enlarging on the degeneracy of the Jews, the Negroes, on
the horrifying secret rituals of the Catholic Church, on the
dangers of miscegenation, on the British-Israel theories.

"Now I will be damned," said Hackett. "The things people
fall for—"

Mendoza said with a short laugh, "There was that folding
table, you know. I'll bet you he presided over meetings of

this nasty little outfit in the back room of that store. But I do wonder how Miss McLennan found out about it."

When Hackett got home he found Angel just taking a casserole out of the oven. She kissed him briskly. "You've really been very good about staying on the maintenance diet, darling. But you're going to fall off it a little tonight because we're in a hurry. And I hope to goodness I can get the children to bed early and they don't get to fussing."

"Where are we going?" asked Hackett amiably.

"No place. I just noticed it in the new *TV Guide*, there's a movie on we want to see. We missed it when it was playing in the theaters, because it was that time Sheila had chickenpox and we couldn't leave her. And it got the rave reviews, it's supposed to be awfully good—that one made on the old Christie mystery, you know, the *Orient Express*."

"Oh, fine," said Hackett. "Just the thing to take my mind off the dirty job, my Angel." He went to strip off tie and jacket.

For a wonder, the children went peaceably to bed, and at eight o'clock the Hacketts settled down on the couch together to watch "Saturday Night at the Movies."

When Mendoza came in at ten o'clock on Sunday morning the office was empty except for Sergeant Lake working a crossword puzzle at the switchboard. "Where is everybody, Jimmy?"

"I think Jase and George went out on the Patterson thing again, and there was a new one down, Art and Tom are on that—body in a car at the County Courthouse parking lot."

"*¡No me diga!* Has somebody killed a judge at last?"

Lake grinned. "I couldn't say. Henry and John are out looking for heisters."

"So you can put me through to the local feds." Mendoza went on into his office and two minutes later was talking to the FBI office in Hollywood.

One of the feds came over, a fellow named Grady, and looked through the stacks of leaflets Mendoza had brought back yesterday. He looked at it sadly; he was a young man, but like any other cop he knew about human nature.

"This outfit," he said distastefully, poking his finger at a pamphlet entitled "Race Purity or the End of Civilization!" "Well, it's on the subversive list, but we don't do much about it—there's not much to do—at least they don't go throwing bombs, and as far as we know they haven't started to stockpile machine guns yet. Just distribute the hate literature and hold secret meetings—get together to exchange passwords and tell each other how superior they are."

"Yes," said Mendoza. "The bandar-log."

"How's that?"

"Mr. Kipling's bandar-log. 'We are the greatest people in the jungle, we know it is true because all of us say it is true!' "

"Oh," said Grady. "It makes you tired to see people being such fools. We all come all shapes and sizes, good, bad and indifferent. You'd think a look at history would tell anybody that. These people, the ones who fall for this junk, they're usually little unimportant people, failures in life, and they need something to prop themselves up, you know? They're a far cry from the real terrorists and propagandists using the hate to create dissension, spread confusion, aiming for the cold communist takeover. They're kind of pathetic people really—but hate is hate."

"Isn't it the truth," said Mendoza. "Well, I suppose this gives us an answer to our particular little puzzle. Parmenter annoyed one of the local brotherhood—maybe he was Grand High Panjandrum and somebody wanted the job—and the brother put him out of the way."

"It's very possible. They don't tend to be very well balanced people, of course. But I guess both of us have had enough to do with the nuts to know how they react."

Mendoza settled back for a desultory discussion of the vagaries of human nature, quite unaware of the storm that was about to break over the office.

Hackett and Landers had gone out on yet another routine

call, a dead body: what Robbery-Homicide was there to deal with. It was a rather queer place to find a body, but the civic center with all its public buildings was surrounded by the inner city, the oldest part of L.A. and some of the shabbiest, and many things happen in the inner city on Saturday nights. They drove the little way to the County Courthouse and found the squad in the parking lot, which held just one car. Barrett was waiting for them.

"I noticed the car because, of course, it's the only one in the lot. I thought it might be on the hot list, so I came up to look, and there he is. And I'll tell you something funny, he looks sort of familiar," said Barrett. "What you can see of him."

"Oh?" Hackett went to take a look. The car was a nearly new Chevrolet hard-top, bright silver. The body was on the passenger side in front, but slumped over sideways. Hackett went around to the driver's side to get a better look at its face. They'd have to get the lab out before they could touch the car or examine the corpse, so they put in a call and Scarne came out with Horder in a mobile unit.

They dusted the right-hand door, lifted a few latents, and got it open. The morgue wagon was standing by then. At least, up here on a Sunday morning, there was nobody around to make up a gawking crowd. They took some pictures and Scarne said, "He looks familiar. Okay, that should do it. Let's see if there's any I.D. on him," and he reached in and yanked the body more upright. It flopped up, still a little rigid, and the head fell back against the seat. The corpse had been a striking-looking man, a big man with broad shoulders, thick black hair slightly waving in front, strongly marked features —broad brow, jutting straight nose, a wide mobile mouth. He looked to be in his late thirties or early forties.

"My good God!" said Hackett. "It's Upchurch. Senator Upchurch."

"I'll be damned if it isn't," said Landers. "What the hell is he doing here?"

"Up—" said Scarne, and stared. "My God. It is. I was

going to vote for him. How'd he get down here, for God's sake?"

Howard Upchurch was a very new figure in national politics, and by all the signs he had been marked for success. He had currently been serving a fourth term in the state senate, and was campaigning for the nomination at the primaries in June to challenge the senior senator for California. He had been, according to the polls, the odds-on favorite to get that nomination.

"I saw him on a TV spot just last night," said Hackett.

They had all seen the news stories, the campaign publicity. Upchurch was running as a common-sensible moderate, with a strong base of Family, Patriotism and Morality. He was described as a solid family man himself, he had been a successful lawyer before entering politics, and he was identified with agricultural interests; he represented a constituency far north in the state where large ranch holdings dominated the local scene. They had all seen the TV spots, heard his well-modulated voice making the pitch. But it wouldn't matter now how many votes he'd have gotten; he wasn't going to Washington next January.

There wasn't any visible mark to say how he had died.

"I'll be damned," said Scarne in sole comment, and rather gingerly began to feel in the pockets. Upchurch was wearing a well-tailored gray suit, white shirt, a discreet dark tie. There was a gold seal ring on his right hand, and a Masonic tie pin fastened to the tie. "Well, he wasn't rolled," said Scarne, handing the billfold to Hackett. There was a hundred and seventy dollars in it, and the plastic slots were crammed with I.D.: credit cards, membership cards for the Elks, Kiwanis, Rotary. Scarne was into other pockets now. He came up with a florists' card, the kind attached to a formal arrangement. In green ink was printed on it *To welcome you to the Beverly Hills Hotel. Compliments of the manager.* Next came a note crumpled hastily into the left jacket pocket.

It was a sheet torn from an interoffice memo pad, and it was headed in scarlet block print, *From the office of Bernard*

Seton. In an overlarge scrawl below that was, *Dear Howie,
suggest we get together for a confab re the campaign and
Tuesday speech, my hotel room, this afternoon—sorry can't
join for dinner, will take rain check. Bernie.* That seemed to
be all that was in the pockets, except for a bunch of keys.

"Well, this is going to make some headlines," said Hackett.
"We'll have the press around."

Landers sniffed and said, "One politician less."

"It's a Hertz car, did you notice?" said Scarne. The keys
were in the ignition.

"He was evidently staying at the Beverly Hills Hotel," said
Hackett. "I suppose we start there. And, hell, it's Sunday, I
don't suppose there'd be anybody at his Sacramento office."

The lab would tow in the car and Upchurch would be delivered to the morgue. There wasn't any obvious injury, and
he could have died of a heart attack, only what was he doing
at the County Courthouse? But whatever, they had to work it.
Hackett and Landers drove out to the Beverly Hills Hotel.

It was an old and still very good hotel, not as large or as
classy as the newer Hilton, the Century-Plaza. And of course
there wasn't going to be any way to avoid the publicity on
this. Hackett asked the desk clerk whether Senator Upchurch
was registered. The desk clerk beamed at him cordially and
agreed that he was. He was a thin dark man with obsequious
eyes and an anxious smile. "I'm sorry to tell you," said Hackett,
bringing out the badge, "that he's just been found dead, and
we'll have to make some inquiries."

The smile vanished. "D-dead!" said the clerk. "Oh, my God!
Oh, my God!"

"We'd like to see his room," said Hackett. "And do you
have a Bernard Seton registered?" The clerk shook his head
dumbly. "All right, let's see the register."

"Really, there's no Seton—"

"I don't doubt it," said Hackett, "but I don't recall where
Upchurch comes from, and I want his home address."

"It's S-San S-S-Sallitas," said the clerk. "Oh, my God. What
—what did he die of?"

"We don't know yet. Will you take us to his room, please. Would you know what time he went out, when he was last seen here?"

Dumbly the clerk took down some keys from behind the desk. "I go—off duty at six. Bob Logan's on—up to midnight. I saw the senator come in—yesterday—about five o'clock. That's all I know."

"All right, thanks."

They rode up to the top floor, and the clerk let them into a room at the end of the corridor. Hackett shut the door on him and they looked around. In ten minutes Landers said, "I'll bet you he was just down here to make a speech, he wasn't intending to stay long." There was only one suitcase, and it held four clean shirts, two folded ties and four sets of clean underwear, four pairs of socks. There was a dark navy suit hanging in the closet, his razor in the bathroom, a few toilet articles on the shelf there. The register said he had checked in on Friday. And a laundry bag in the closet held a little pile of dirty clothes, two shirts, two sets of underwear, two pairs of socks.

The only other objects in the room were a copy of *Playboy*, a pamphlet about the aims and methods of the League of Women Voters and a lot of campaign material from the Upchurch for Senate Committee. Landers picked up one of the brochures and read it, shook his head and passed it to Hackett. Upchurch was firmly outspoken, it announced proudly, in support of the sanctity of the American family, law and order, the protection of the American consumer, the necessity to strengthen and broaden our economy, the improvement of education for the younger generation, and the reaffirmation of the eternal principles of democratic government.

"The usual vague hogwash. We're supposed to have a republic, not a democracy. See B. Franklin."

Hackett laughed. "The language degenerating, Tom, too many people don't know the difference. We'd better go back to the office to do any phoning." And they'd only been in there about forty minutes, but it was long enough; by the time they got down to the lobby the press was just arriving. The desk clerk had called in the scoop.

They were annoyed, and ran the gauntlet out to the car. The press would be besieging the office and Mendoza would have a fit.

Back at base, Hackett was stymied by Information, who informed him that the number he desired was unlisted and could not be given out. "This is the police," said Hackett. Information was sorry, but she had no proof of that and was not allowed to give out unlisted numbers. "Give me your supervisor," said Hackett, and had a long argument with that one before he got her to call him back, verify the claim and read him the number. He dialed and let it ring twelve times; nobody answered.

"I suppose there might be somebody in his office," said Landers. "Height of a political campaign, likely there'll be an army of people there stuffing envelopes begging for money."

Hackett got the Senate Office Building in Sacramento, and the phone rang four times before an impatient voice answered. "Is this Senator Upchurch's office?" asked Hackett.

"Yes, sir, what can we do for you, sir?"

"This is the police in Los Angeles. I'm—"

"Police? What's wrong? Is anything the matter with the senator? I'm his secretary, Martin Unger, you can tell me anything in perfect confidence, I assure you, I'm quite familiar with—"

"I'm sorry to have to tell you that the senator's just been found dead." Hackett started to go on to ask how to contact the family, explain about the handling of the body, but Unger didn't let him.

He just said in a startled wail, "Dead? Dead!" And then the line crashed down at the other end, and hummed emptily.

Grace and Higgins had been wandering around all day trying to find out who might have seen Edna Patterson last. An autopsy wasn't going to pin down any exact time. She could have been killed anytime on Tuesday, since the refuse truck came early and nobody remembered seeing her take her can back to the garage. Linda Gilman had told them where she usually shopped, given the names of her closest friends; she'd kept her address book in a drawer of the phone table and it was gone with everything else.

A market clerk at Von's remembered seeing her at about four o'clock on Monday afternoon. She'd talked to a casual friend on the phone at seven o'clock Monday night. For a while that looked as if that was it; they tried six or seven other places and people, but nobody remembered seeing her, talking to her, since the week before.

Then they found a salesclerk at a drugstore who had seen her on Tuesday morning. Mrs. Patterson didn't drive, and shopped close to home, along Vernon, along Hoover. The clerk volunteered that Mrs. Patterson hadn't looked so good.

In the midst of all the legwork, they were also wondering if that rapist would hit again, with a new victim in mind for this nice April Sunday. And wondering where Eileen Mooney's body was. When it was found—if it was found— there might be some evidence on it to tie in Rudy Bartovic, or there might not.

After they'd stopped for lunch they tried another close friend, a woman named Agnes Sherman, who used to live around here and had attended the same church, but had gone to live with her son and his wife after she'd had a heart attack. They hadn't, said Linda Gilman, seen each other often anymore, but used to talk on the phone. Mrs. Sherman lived in Redondo Beach. "Pity to give her another heart attack, breaking the news," said Grace. So when he called, he just told her he was calling for Mrs. Gilman, who wanted to know if she had talked to Mrs. Patterson lately, and when.

"Why, is she worse?" asked an anxious voice. "Yes, I talked to her on Wednesday morning, and she had a bad cold coming on, said she wasn't going to church that night. Is she all right? What—who is this?"

What a tangled web, thought Grace: and just trying to be

133

diplomatic. He asked to talk to her son, and explained it to him. Let him take it from there.

He'd been using a pay phone at the restaurant where they'd had lunch; he went back to the table where Higgins was finishing another cup of coffee, sat down and said, "I've just had a brainwave." He told Higgins about Mrs. Sherman. "We said nobody would murder the woman for her furniture, but how do you like the idea that it was never meant to be a murder at all, just a nice neat pro burglary? And whoever planned it knew enough about her to think she'd be at church on Wednesday night? And then they walked in and found her home?"

"Now you just may have something there," said Hackett. "The back door wasn't locked. She wasn't feeling well, she could have overlooked a thing like that. And then, having killed her to shut her up, they thought they might as well be hung for a sheep as a lamb."

"It did look like a pro job," said Grace, "so the lab may not give us anything."

They went back to the office, and were surprised to find the press swarming around.

On this peaceful Sunday afternoon, Alison was sitting in the living room brooding over brochures and estimated prices on the concrete-block wall: she had seen two firms about it yesterday. Ken Kearney had started energetically to erect his wire-and-post fence, which looked like something out of a concentration camp, but it was a large house and he still had a long way to go. The Five Graces, meantime, were mournfully occupying the corral.

During lunch El Señor had proudly brought in a very large, very dead field mouse, and Alison and Mairí had sent an SOS to Ken, who had just gotten back to work after his own lunch. "A dead bird, now, I can just do something with," confessed Mairí, "but mice I canna abide."

The twins had been riding for a short while this morning, and after lunch had wandered off, probably to watch Ken digging postholes. Except for the monotonous sound of his vigorous hammering, the house was peaceful, and Alison leaped up quivering as he let out a roar just outside the open window.

"For God's sweet sake! Here, you, get out of that! Damn it to hell— Johnny! Terry! You pair of young devils, I'll scalp you—"

Alison rushed to the window. "What's happened?"

Kearney turned a flushed angry face to her, and just pointed. "I told that pair to stay out of the corral, that latch is damned stiff. If I hadn't run out of staples just now—"

"Oh, my Lord!" said Alison. All the while he'd been busily building fence around the other side of the house, the Five Graces had been enjoying the expensive landscaping on this side. Another Italian cypress tree was denuded, and several hibiscus shrubs. "I'll *murder* them!" said Alison, making for the door. "Johnny! Terry!"

". . . And I couldn't get anybody to answer the damn phone again," said Hackett, "and nobody answers Upchurch's home phone, and we've been stymied. Evidently he was going to make this speech on Tuesday, but—" Higgins, Grace, and Mendoza were listening to the tale of frustration interestedly. "We don't know who this Bernard Seton is or who else Upchurch may have come here to see—"

"Why not ask the press?" said Mendoza. "They ought to know. A politician would want advance publicity."

"It was the first thing we thought of, damn it," said Landers. Detective work could be boring and frustrating, but it was even more frustrating to have it there to do and be unable to get on with it. "He was going to make a speech to the League of Women Voters on Tuesday, in San Diego, and we got hold of the chairman or whatever, but she didn't know what his schedule was up here." It was three o'clock and they hadn't got anywhere on this all day; and Landers didn't much like politicians. "The only damn thing we've found out is that he flew in from Sacramento on Friday, and picked up a Hertz car at the airport. He already had a reservation at the hotel."

"If we knew who this Seton is, he'd probably know something. They don't know anything at the hotel. He was out all day yesterday, came in about five and went out again a little later, and that's the last they saw of him."

"*¡Ca!*" said Mendoza, brushing his mustache.

Palliser looked in with Glasser behind him. "Conference on your politician? We had to wade through the press. You'll be glad to know we just cleared one—the big fat Negro with the big gun. He was the last one out of Records, of course, but he's scared of cops and came apart right away. We've just applied for the warrant. What happened to the politician?"

"We don't know yet," said Mendoza. "I can't raise anybody in Bainbridge's office."

"I can't resist quoting Hilaire Belloc," said Palliser. "You know the one. 'Here richly, with ridiculous display, The politician's corpse was laid away; While all of his acquaintance sneered and slanged, I wept—for I had longed to see him hanged.' "

"Oh, that's very nice," said Landers in the general laughter. As it died, a man came rushing into the office like a scalded cat. He was a young man in very natty brown sports clothes, with a shock of wild blond hair and flashing blue eyes. Lake was behind him looking outraged.

"I had to give a statement to the press downstairs," said the young man rapidly, "and I hope to God you won't foul me up by saying something different. I said he was seriously ill and would cancel all engagements until— You don't really mean he's *dead?* I came as soon as I could get a flight—"

"Mr. Unger?" said Hackett. "Good. Yes, of course he's dead, as I told you. No, we don't know of what yet. There'll be an autopsy. His wife ought to be informed, I couldn't get any—"

"They're in Europe. The whole family. I sent a cable," said Unger. "Oh, my God, gentlemen, you don't understand what a goddamned awful thing this is!" He ignored the chair Mendoza offered him; he ran a hand through his wild hair, and there was a sudden sob in his voice. "You—who didn't know him—don't realize what a terrible, terrible loss to our country this is! Howard Upchurch was the finest man I ever knew, the most honorable patriot I ever met. It was foregone he'd have won the nomination, and become our new junior senator, and who knows, gentlemen, after a few terms in the Senate he might have ended in the White House. He was most certainly potential presidential timber. I simply can't believe this terrible thing—"

"Now just calm down, Mr. Unger, you'll have to answer some questions," said Hackett.

"Certainly, certainly, any way I can help you— Oh, God, the problems this is going to make—poor darling Nora Upchurch, such a dear woman and they were so devoted—"

Lake was gesturing wildly at Mendoza over the babble, and Mendoza went out to the corridor. "It's Harbor," said Lake in a dropped voice. "They've just pulled a body in, past the Long Beach breakwater."

"And it's hardly the lesser of two evils," said Mendoza hardly. "But let Art deal with that—that—"

"Lackey," said Lake, unexpectedly.

"What did they say?"

"Well, they don't think anybody could identify it," said Lake unhappily.

"*Dios.* I probably won't be back," said Mendoza, and went to get his hat.

He looked at the thing lying there in the morgue tray, and it was a very ugly thing, but he had seen a lot of ugly things like it. He said, "You'll have had some experience, what do you think?"

"Well, God," said the Harbor precinct man, and scratched his head. Harbor patrolled in boats, not squad cars. "What happens in the ocean, it makes times damn difficult. The fish, you know. This one, it could have been out there four-five days or four-five weeks. But you wanted to know about any female corpses, and I'd take an oath that's female, by the size and all."

Mendoza thought of that photograph of Eileen Mooney, the pert red-blonde with the tip-tilted freckled nose. There wasn't any hair left on this thing, there wasn't much but a skeleton and withered flesh, and if it was Eileen there wasn't going to be any way to nail Rudy Bartovic for it, and he felt coldly savage about that.

"Dental records," said the Harbor man.

"Yes. Obviously the only way we'll get identification. I'll get back to you on it," said Mendoza.

It was the beginning of rush-hour traffic, and the freeway was jammed. He got held up at the Stack where he got off the San Diego Freeway, but he got to the apartment on Clinton at six-twenty. "Oh—" said Rose Mooney. "Oh—is there —is there anything—"

"Miss Mooney," said Mendoza, "I just don't know. What I came to ask is what dentist your sister went to."

"D-dentist. Dr. Westfall on Sunset Boulevard. Why? Why?" Her eyes widened in fear.

They knew, now, about the background of the Mooney girls. Orphans, the parents killed in an accident, and raised by elderly grandparents who were both dead now. Two nice girls, making a life together, and then the stupid irrational punk like Bartovic—

He said, "There's a body. We don't know that it's Eileen. There's only one way to be sure."

"Oh—my—God," she said dully. "Oh, no—"

"Now it might not be," he said.

She huddled on the couch, her head down. She said thickly, "Yes, I know." And there was a sudden rattle at the door, and her gaze fixed over his shoulder, and she screamed. *"Eileen—"*

"Yes, darling, here we are—surprise, surprise!"

SEVEN

"Where have you been? And what's Randy—"

"Why, what do you— Darling, we sent you a wire! Do you mean to say— They swore you'd get it by five o'clock, of course I knew you'd worry when I didn't come to work, so you could tell Mr. Fox too— Didn't you get it?"

"You left— All that— Everybody thought Rudy Bartovic had kidnaped you and m-murdered— He just came to tell me they'd found your body—"

"What?"

"Your tote bag—with all the blood—and you didn't come home—the police have been looking and looking, and I was so scared—"

They turned blank gazes on Mendoza, and he said, "And just what did happen to you, Miss Mooney?" She was even prettier than her picture, the copper-blond hair in a flip short-cut, the tip-tilted nose impudent with its freckles. He was a stocky young fellow with a square amiable face, genial blue eyes, sandy hair.

"*Not* Miss Mooney, it's Mrs. Penner!" She held out her

left hand proudly to show. "You mean you *never got it?* You didn't know? Whatever *do* you—"

"The police—everybody thought— They had Rudy in jail but— All the things in the park, it looked as if—"

They both started to laugh hysterically. "Oh, darling! Oh, dear, I know it's really not funny, but we couldn't know you wouldn't get the wire, how could we? I'm as sorry as I can be, but it's all right now, isn't it? You see, we'd both been so miserable, and of course I knew Randy would come back and apologize—and of course he knew I liked to sit in the park, and so when he came that morning—I suppose Mrs. Lally just didn't see him—and I wasn't there, he came down to the park—"

"Oh, my God!" he said, choking on laughter. "The blood! Oh, my God, that's funny—the *police*—a murder—" They were giggling helplessly. He pulled himself together with an effort. "I'd had this accident at work—I work at the big Sears warehouse on Olympic—case of glasses fell down and I got this bad cut on my arm—reason I was off work—" He pulled off his jacket, and still had a bandage on his left arm. Suddenly he doubled over again, laughing. "That blood! The police! Looking for a body! Oh, my God!"

"Darling!" she said. "You see, he came, and we made up—" They beamed at each other fatuously.

"My lucky day. I'd just won a thousand bucks on a horse, and I'm not usually good with the ponies—"

"And I promised to marry him if he swore solemnly he'd never bet more than five dollars on anything ever again. So we decided just to go and *do it*—"

"Oh, my God!" he said. "The police thinking—" They were both highly amused. "Well, we were clinching each other, we were both pretty excited, we'd sat down right there, and I knocked my arm against the tree and started the damn thing bleeding again. By the time I noticed it, it'd made a little mess. I just tied my handkerchief around it—"

"And just why didn't you come home for some clothes?"

asked Mendoza coldly. "If, as I gather—"

"Oh, that was my fault. I said we'd just live it up and have a blowout, damn the money, maybe we'd never have that much to blow again, and we'd get clothes over there. We didn't have to stay at a fancy place, but make it a honeymoon to remember—so we just drove up to the airport and got the eleven-o'clock flight to Vegas—"

"And I was so excited I never *thought* about my knitting—oh, it's all too silly! And we got a suitcase and new clothes and everything in Vegas, and we were married that night—and of course we thought you knew all about it! We didn't know how long we'd stay, so I didn't tell you that, but *of course* we thought—"

"Well," said Mendoza, brushing his mustache. "All's well that ends well, but I do hope you both realize that you've cost us a good deal of time, work, and taxpayers' money. We really thought we had a homicide to work."

They went into gales of laughter again, and Penner controlled himself to say contritely, "We're very sorry, sir—but my God, of all the ridiculous—that blood—oh, God!"

"Well," said Rose shortly, looking at them with cold eyes. "I'm going to call Western Union." She looked up the number and dialed, explained, waited a long time while they checked records, and finally said, "I see. Well, thank you . . . They couldn't get anyone to answer the phone. I was over at Mrs. Lally's—we were just wild, of course, worrying. The police were hunting for Bartovic and looking for your body— And of course they don't deliver telegrams by hand anymore. They sent it by mail. On Wednesday."

This was the culmination of the joke. They broke down again, leaning on each other in helpless mirth. "The m-m-mail!" wailed Eileen. "You'll p-probably get it tomorrow—Oh, darling, I *am* sorry but it's such a scream—"

"That *blood*," he said happily. "Police out looking—oh, my God—"

Mendoza went out to the Ferrari and started home. Eileen

was a very nice girl, but at the moment he could have murdered her himself. At home, after a belated and warmed-over dinner, he called the night watch and gave them the news.

And of course on Monday morning everybody was interested to hear about that, and did some cussing and laughing about it. Overnight, by the description, the hair-trigger heister had pulled another job—he hadn't gotten much loot on the last one—at a movie house down on Main; the ticket seller would be coming in to make a statement. At least, as far as they knew, the rapist hadn't been out again yesterday. And Martin Unger, said Hackett, had told them who Bernard Seton was: a representative of the public relations firm managing the political campaign for Upchurch. "He's staying at the Beverly Hilton, but I couldn't raise him last night up to eleven, and he's probably not up yet."

"Yes," said Mendoza, "and we still don't know whether the man died of a heart attack or what." He took up the phone and told Lake to get him Bainbridge's office. Bainbridge came on himself.

"Well, I was very sorry to hear about it, when I came in yesterday. Upchurch had impressed me as a very sound man, I was going to vote for him. I wonder what in hell could have happened to him."

"Well, that's what I called to ask you, Doctor."

"Oh. Well, I haven't done the autopsy yet, but as far as cause of death goes, there's not much doubt about what I'll find. Depressed skull fracture. Bang on the head—however it happened—you can feel it under the hair just behind the right temple. Probably sometime on Saturday night, yes. It could have been caused by a fall on some hard surface—could have been an accident, of course. I'll be able to tell you more later."

Mendoza relayed that. "By that note, Seton saw Upchurch sometime on Saturday afternoon, and may have known where he intended to go that evening. And there's also this great white brotherhood bunch; if possible I suppose we should try to find which brother took Parmenter off. There's enough to do." Hackett and Landers went out, and Mendoza listened to Grace's conclusions on the Patterson case, agreed with them. Higgins could wait for the ticket seller. Grace went down to SID to see if the lab had anything for them yet.

The ticket seller came in at nine o'clock, a luscious dark girl named Maria Ortiz. The movie house was a big one, running exclusively Mexican films, and usually drew a full audience at night; the heister had gotten away with around a hundred and fifty bucks. She described the heister graphically. "He was very big, he had light hair, oh, rough and long"— she touched the lobe of her ear—"and he was very sure of himself, very confident, you know? I was frightened, I had never seen a gun so close before, and at first I didn't know what to do—and when I didn't open the register he put the gun closer to me and he said it again in Spanish—give me the money."

"Oh, really?" said Mendoza, interested.

She nodded. "It wasn't *good* Spanish, you know, but understandable. He said, *Deme la moneda, chica.*"

She signed the statement and Higgins filed it away. He said, "Well, if he is one of these jokers we heard about from NCIC, somebody should know if one of them speaks bastard Spanish. But if you ask me that singles out this Leroy Rogers. He's originally from Texas, and there's a lot of coming and going over that border. Rogers is wanted in Atlanta, but I don't know if they've got his whole record on file." He got on the phone to Atlanta; a Captain Moreau told him that Rogers had been fingered by the pal who'd pulled the job with him, he hadn't any record with them, and he was also wanted for a bank heist in Dallas, where most of his record had been piled up. Higgins called Dallas, where a Lieutenant Fitzwilliam pulled Rogers' record and confirmed that he spoke some Spanish. They had a mug shot and would wire a copy immediately.

"And probably," said Higgins, "if we do pick him up, Atlanta will have priority, damn it. But come to think, Georgia still has the death penalty in force, doesn't it?"

Grace came back and said that SID had picked up a lot of latents in the Patterson house, and was still processing them; they had gotten all the family's prints for comparison, and it might take a while.

"It's a great tragedy, of course," said Bernard Seton. "The loss of a very able man, who'd have been a credit to our government, I'm sure." He looked at Hackett and Landers firmly, very much in control of the situation, which was something of a feat under the circumstances. He had been caught completely off base when they knocked at his door ten minutes ago; he hadn't heard of Upchurch's death; and he was just out of bed, unshaven, and wearing a bathrobe over pajamas. For about thirty seconds he had been startled and shaken, and then some inward automatic mechanism had operated to erect the smooth façade. "A very mysterious accident, it seems to be."

"We're still investigating," said Hackett. "We found a note from you in his pocket. Could you tell us—"

"Oh, yes," said Seton. He was a very sleek product: about forty, tall and lean, with a lantern jaw and swift dark eyes, the dark coloring that would make a second shave necessary if he was going out of an evening. He sat in the one armchair in this untidy colorless hotel room with the unmade bed behind him, talking easily up at the two standing detectives, and explained the position carelessly. His firm, Douglas-Hocking Public Relations, handled all kinds of publicity matters as well as political campaigns. "The days are gone, you know, when politicians wrote their own speeches and went around kissing babies, a good campaign needs professional planning and management. I was out here—our headquarters are in Chicago, of course—to evaluate how Upchurch's campaign was going, attend a few speeches, but I had a few other clients to see for the firm on other business, as long as I was here. Upchurch had come to Los Angeles primarily to tape an interview for a TV program, a public service thing called

'Meet the Candidates,' I suppose you've heard of it. Then he had this speech in San Diego on Tuesday, and he was flying back to Sacramento that night. Yes, I knew he'd be at this big Rotary meeting at eight A.M. on Saturday morning, I'd arranged it—it was in one of the banquet rooms here— God," and he shuddered, "deliver me from Rotarians, the hearty breakfast meetings! However. I left that note for him there, I had an appointment later that morning."

"And did you see him that afternoon?"

"Yes, he came here about one-thirty Saturday afternoon." Seton had ordered coffee sent up, and sat sipping it; he had offered some to Hackett and Landers, politely. "We sat and talked for a couple of hours. I made a few suggestions about getting important points across, and so on—not important now—oh, it was all on a perfectly friendly basis—and he left around three-thirty, I think."

"Do you know what his plans were for the rest of the day?" asked Landers.

Seton gave him a friendly smile. "Do you know," he said, "you really don't look old enough to be a detective, Mr. Landers. Or maybe I'm just getting on myself. Well, that's why I can't quite understand why he was found where he was. As far as I know he intended to go out to dinner, go back to his hotel and spend the evening going over his speech." They had found the typescript of the speech in Upchurch's hotel room, yesterday. "And you see, he wasn't at all familiar with Los Angeles, he didn't know anyone here, and he asked me about restaurants. He liked French cuisine, and I suggested the restaurant right here, L'Escoffier, and La Bella Fontana at the Beverly Wilshire, Chez Claude, François's or Jimmy's in Beverly Hills. He said they all sounded fine, and did I know a place called the Granada at the Century-Plaza, somebody had recommended it to him, and I told him I'd never been there but it was probably good, that was a good hotel. He was going back to clean up a little, and then going to a restaurant, that's all I could tell you."

"That's the last you saw of him? Well, thanks very much."

"You know something," said Landers as they waited for the elevator, "we ought to have some of that campaign literature, Art. There's a good picture of him splashed all over all of it. If we're going to be asking about him at these restaurants, it'd be useful."

"Occasionally you use your brains, Tom," said Hackett. "Let's go and get some." They went back to the Beverly Hills Hotel about ten blocks away, got the keys to Upchurch's room from a subdued desk clerk and abstracted a handful of the campaign brochures with Upchurch's virile, trustworthy, smiling photograph prominently displayed. As they came out the front entrance and turned toward the parking lot, Hackett said, "Wait a minute. They've got valet parking here, haven't they? Separate parking accommodation for guests' cars. I just wonder. If the attendant happened to notice which way he turned out, or if he asked directions, it might give us a clue where he did go."

They found the private hotel parking lot around at one side, and the attendant lounging there in a canvas chair in the shade of the building, reading a sports magazine. Hackett showed him the badge and explained. "Say," he said interestedly, "I heard something on the grapevine about some big shot we had staying here dropping dead or something." He was a lank young man with a very deep tan. "Tell me what car he was driving and I might remember something." Hackett handed him one of the leaflets. "This him? Oh-oh, sure. He had a renter. Gee, he's a good-looking guy, isn't he? Yeah, I remember him some. He showed up about two-thirty on Friday afternoon, and went in the hotel, and then about five-thirty the desk called and he wanted the car brought around to the front entrance. It was just before I was due to go off, I'm here until six and then Chuck comes on."

"Fine," said Hackett. "Do you remember about Saturday? Happen to notice which way he turned out of the lot when he left, about five or five-thirty?"

The attendant shook his head. "Sorry, I'm not on on Saturdays. Him on Friday I remember. I brought the car up to the front steps, and this guy was there with a cute little blond chick maybe twenty, really stacked—they were laughing and talking, and he gave me a buck and I walked back to the lot and that was it."

Hinted at, Hackett gave him a dollar. They started back to the car. Landers said darkly, "The devoted family man—hah. He gets here on Friday afternoon, doesn't know a soul in L.A., and three hours later he's picked up a pretty dolly to play with. For God's sake. And I wonder where?"

"By what the fellow said, the car wasn't out until then, after he checked in. It could have been at the bar here, I suppose. But that won't be open until two o'clock. I don't know about these other restaurants, but we can go and ask."

"Politicians!" said Landers.

The wire photo came in about ten-thirty, and Higgins took it to show the Ortiz girl and she identified it, so he took it to Clyde Burroughs and he identified it. "Why didn't you show me this one in the first place?" he asked indignantly. So now they knew that their hair-trigger heister was Leroy Rogers, but they had no idea what car he was driving, where he was living or where he might hit next. Higgins came back to the office. Mendoza was closeted with a couple of feds, Grace was talking about babies with Wanda, showing her the latest pictures of plump brown Celia Anne. There were other heisters to look for and Glasser was probably out on that.

"Oh, the autopsy report on Barker came in," said Grace. "There's not much in it."

There wasn't, except that it sounded like the same knife. "That," said Higgins abstractedly, "is a very queer thing."

He thought about Rogers. That heist job in Atlanta—when had it been?—he'd taken some notes, talking on the phone; he looked them up and checked. The date had been March 4, and Atlanta had picked up the pal on the eleventh and he had fingered Rogers, but Atlanta couldn't find him. He could have landed here anytime between then and his first job here, and he wouldn't have had much money; they hadn't made a big haul on the Atlanta job. He wouldn't have bought a car. He could have stolen one in another state, but there was no way to find out about that. Or he could have stolen one here. He passed on all that to Grace. "It just occurs to me," he said thoughtfully, massaging his craggy jaw, "just to be on the safe side, because he seems to be very handy with that Colt, it might be a good idea to brief all the Traffic men to use extreme caution in approaching any car in this area. Or any out-of-state cars."

"I think," said Grace, "that is a dandy idea—just to be on the safe side."

Higgins started downstairs to see the watch commander in Traffic. At least all the Traffic shifts would be briefed, beginning with the swing at four o'clock.

Mendoza had been pessimistic about the proposed trap for the brotherhood. "Damn it, the rest of them would know he's dead, nobody's going to show up at that place again."

"We don't know," said Grady patiently. "It's very possible they don't know, that is, aside from the one who killed him. I'll say this, Mendoza. These people—one of the ways they get their kicks is the secrecy of the whole thing. Like the little boys' secret clubs, you know? They're unimportant people, as I said, having to pretend to be important, and the idea that they're part of a secret group of superior beings provides a big thrill. They tend to stay away from each other except for the secret meetings—and your man's murder wasn't spread all over the papers, if it was mentioned at all."

"True."

"Now we don't know when they met, or how often. But Carroll here has been doing some research on what we know about this outfit, and most of the local groups seem to meet about every couple of weeks, on week nights. That might not apply to this one—who knows?—but we can give it a try."

So they were sitting here, on three of Mr. Parmenter's folding chairs, in the back room of Mr. Parmenter's pharmacy, at eight o'clock on Monday night, Mendoza and the two feds.

They had put on all the lights in front and left the door unlocked. Mendoza, feeling rather sleepy, had just worked it out that Parmenter had probably left the lights on until everybody had gathered and then turned them off for the secret meeting, which was the only reason that Rauschman had been able to notice them, when Carroll beside him tensed and put a hand on his arm. Somebody was walking in the front door.

They waited, and whoever it was came down the store and around the corner toward the back room. "Gregory?" said a fretful voice.

"Come right in," said Grady cordially. He had his gun in one hand and his badge in the other. It was a little rabbit-faced man who stared at them and suddenly looked ready to faint. "Do sit down," said Grady; they had set out a few chairs just in case. The little man seemed transfixed, and sat down meekly under the gun. Somebody else came in, and this one turned out to be a tall weedy kid about nineteen; he tried to put up a halfhearted fight, and Grady shoved him into a chair roughly. The third one was an elderly man with a limp, and then they waited for five minutes with nobody saying anything, until the door opened again out there, and by the footsteps two men came in.

Without warning the rabbity man made a dive for Grady's gun arm and shouted an inarticulate warning. Not expecting it, Grady stumbled against the chair. The footsteps out there began to run, and the two feds ran too, and Mendoza pulled out his own gun to hold the ones they had.

"That wasn't very sportsmanlike," he said to the rabbit. "I thought you people went in for all the high principles."

"One can't fight evil with fair tactics," said the rabbit smartly. "How did you know where to come? And where is Gregory?" As a matter of fact he was still at the morgue, because no one quite knew what to do with him; there wasn't a soul to arrange a funeral.

Grady and Carroll came back emptyhanded and Grady said shortly, "So this is the bag. Those two looked just a little more important from the back view, one of them a big fellow, but they had a start and they made it around the corner to a car, I heard it start up. What a haul."

"Listen," said the kid unhappily, "it's only my second time here, I don't know much about—"

The other two looked at him disapprovingly. "Oh, come on, let's see what we've got," said Carroll tiredly.

They didn't have much. The kid was Jim Ferguson, a student at LACC. He said old Parmenter had given him some stuff to read, it had been kind of interesting, he'd been to one meeting but he hadn't joined yet, and he didn't know there was anything illegal about it.

The elderly man was Richard Cooke, a retired janitor for the Board of Education. At intervals he kept invoking the Fifth Amendment, and aside from that he wouldn't say anything except to ask what they'd done with Parmenter.

The rabbit was Edmund Bond, a salesclerk at a men's shop in Hollywood, and he was relatively voluble. He refused to give them any information about the other local members, but he told them he'd be proud to become a martyr for the cause.

"Are you," asked Mendoza, "the leader or chairman or whatever you call it?"

Unguardedly Bond said, "Oh, no, that—" and shut his mouth.

"That was one of those who got away. I didn't think you looked like leadership material," said Mendoza distastefully. They left them sitting there and went into the front part of the store to discuss it.

The feds had been all over this store and the house without finding anything in the nature of a membership list. Mendoza agreed that very probably Parmenter had supplied the meeting place, but wasn't the local group leader; that one would keep what records were kept, and that one was probably one of the two who had got away.

"Damn it," said Grady, "we can't hold them on anything. As I told you, this bunch doesn't build bombs. Yet."

"You were really obliging me," said Mendoza, "looking for a murderer. *Gracias*. We don't know how many others were just arriving, and got away too."

"But those two back there, the regular members, don't seem to know that Parmenter's dead. If it was one of this bunch who killed him—"

"For a personal and private reason," said Mendoza. "He wouldn't be boasting about it to any of the rest of them, and also, of course, he'd innocently turn up here tonight, to show the rest he didn't know and be all mystified when the place was locked up. And equally, when he spotted the lights on, he'd have stayed away. Altogether an abortive evening."

"No, we haven't helped you much," said Grady. "And we'll let those poor idiots go. You can't change them, that's for sure."

"And I really can't feel," said Mendoza, picking up his hat, "that Mr. Parmenter is any great loss."

At least the electric eye had been installed in the gate today, and tomorrow he'd be driving a loaner while the gadget got installed in the Ferrari.

"And just look at this damned night report!" said Hackett on Tuesday morning. He waved it at Mendoza. "Four new heists, and the boys didn't have time to go out asking questions on Upchurch. Damn it, those hotels have got little bars and restaurants all over, we haven't begun to cover them all yet. I suppose we'll have to do the overtime on it, most of them aren't open till afternoon."

"Yes, business picking up," said Mendoza. It was Grace's day off supposedly, but he had come in, being sent an SOS from the desk. They were missing Nick Galeano. Everybody else was there too, taking quick notes on the night reports, outlining the day's work ahead.

"Morning, Luis." Dr. Bainbridge came waddling in, stouter than ever, with the inevitable black cigar, and took the chair beside Hackett's desk, where Mendoza had perched one hip.

"I knew you'd be anxious to have the details on this one, I did the autopsy myself last night. Press is giving it a play, aren't they?"

"In spades." Not getting anything useful from the police, the press had had to fall back on the highlights of Howard Upchurch's career and public life, and there had been pictures of, an interview with, his attractive wife—who, the press said, was prostrate with shock and grief. Pictures of four handsome children, teen-age on down. The press was calling it a mysterious accident, and Bainbridge repeated that now, rather thoughtfully.

"It's as useful a phrase as any. Wife's good-looking, isn't she? Well"—he sighed—"you want chapter and verse, and I can't give you much. He might have been attacked suddenly, but he hadn't been in a fight, his hands aren't marked. He could have had a sudden hard fall, onto a cement sidewalk or something like that. Just as I told you, he died of a depressed skull fracture—it's just behind the right temple. He might have lived half an hour or an hour, but probably unconscious. Times—well call it between six and ten on Saturday night. He'd had the equivalent of about two double highballs." Bainbridge puffed at his cigar and added mournfully, "Fine healthy specimen, by the way. Man in the prime of life. And he sounded like a very good man, too—kind of man we need more of in Washington, hah? Well, there's your report, and we're busy." He laid the manila folder on Hackett's desk and stumped out.

Landers, who had just cast up his eyes at that, said sardonically, "Man in the prime of life all right, him picking up the blond floozy as soon as he landed here."

"Did you find out any more about that?" asked Mendoza, grinning.

"Well, we asked around in the bar and restaurant there," said Hackett, "but nobody seems to have noticed anything. He could have spotted the girl alone in the bar or somewhere, or she could have been on the make—"

"Or," said Mendoza, "he might have had a date set up

with her, Art. Maybe Seton only thinks Upchurch didn't know anybody here."

"Damn it, we can't do anything until these places are open."

"Preserve patience. You'd better hear what happened last night," and he told them about the brothers.

"I suppose that is the likeliest thing," said Hackett, "that one of them had a private fight with Parmenter. He didn't seem to know anybody else."

Landers just said, "People."

"But you know, Luis, there was a funny feeling about that street that day—I don't know, I couldn't say why. Just a feeling." Hackett sat back and reached for a cigarette.

"That wasn't you I saw driving up in a Chevy a while ago, was it?" asked Landers. Mendoza liked exotic cars, and he could afford the taste, with all the loot his grandfather had left.

Mendoza explained about the electric eye. "I only hope it works," he added, sounding doubtful. "Some of the ideas that girl has had—talk about one thing leading to another— ¡Valgame Dios!"

Of the four new heists, one was Mutt and Jeff again, and this time they had dropped a receipt in the amount of sixty dollars from a motel on Avenue Twenty. The others were all new to the detectives: one description was of a short thin Mexican type, another of a tall thin Negro, and on the fourth there was no description at all: he'd been wearing a stocking mask.

They started to work it as they could. Higgins, Glasser, Grace and Palliser went down to R. and I. and Phil Landers took the descriptions and went away to feed the computer. In half an hour they were handed no fewer than nineteen possible suspects from Records to hunt for, whose descriptions and pedigrees made them at least likely to have pulled these jobs. And that, of course, was leaving out the fourth heist entirely.

Grace, Higgins and Palliser went out to start that legwork.

The addresses in Records for those men might not all be up to date; criminals tended to drift around. They might not find any of them. None of these men might be guilty, this time. But it was a place to start.

Glasser and Wanda drove out to the motel on Avenue Twenty. It was over in Lincoln Heights. It was a ramshackle, ancient place with about twelve little wooden cabins, one of the front ones occupied by the manager. He was a paunchy dark-brown fellow, with a couple of front teeth missing, and he looked at the badge fearfully and said, "Man, we never have no trouble here. All nice an' quiet, I don't let in no junkies or drunks."

"Nobody said you did," said Glasser, and showed him the receipt. "Do you remember these two men?"

"I go look in the book." They went in with him, to a crowded little fusty room with a black-and-white TV blaring. He shut down the sound, found a thick old ledger, leafed back. "Oh, them, yeah," he said. "They was here three nights. Ten a night."

"They each rented a cabin?"

"Naw, naw. There was two couples. Mr. and Mrs. Smith, Mr. and Mrs. Brown. One short fat guy and one tall thin guy."

"What about the women?" asked Wanda.

He shrugged. "I only saw 'em that one time. Just a pair of broads. I couldn't tell you what they looked like."

"What car were they driving? Did you take the plate number?"

"Naw, I don't bother with that. Most people not here very long. I think it was white, a Ford or Chevy or something, I don't know."

"Oh, well," said Glasser as he slid under the Gremlin's wheel, "they're such a pair of bunglers they'll probably get dropped on eventually."

Palliser and Grace had wasted all morning trying to catch up to just one quarry, one Alfonso Marquez, who sounded like one of the likeliest on that heist last night. He had changed jobs, and as soon as he was off parole last month he had changed apartments; and through the vague memories of old neighbors and someone who knew his brother who lived in Glendale, they finally chased down his newest address over in Pasadena. There wasn't anybody home. A man came out of the apartment next door and said, "You lookin' for Al?"

"That's right," said Palliser. "You know where he is?"

"Well, he's in jail," said the man. "The cops picked him up Saturday night for heisting a gas station and I guess he couldn't make bail."

Just to be sure, they checked with the Pasadena jail, and he was there. "This is," said Palliser, "one of the times I wish I'd decided to be an English teacher."

"Dad wanted me to go in for medicine, naturally," said Grace, whose father was a gynecologist. "I never had any ambition that way, but there was a time I thought of the ministry. Believe it or not. Decided I didn't have any real call. And isn't it about time for lunch?"

They had lunch at a place in Pasadena, and started to look for Rafael Torres. Surprisingly, he was where his latest record said he should be, at an address in Boyle Heights, and they brought him back to base to question him. He couldn't tell them where he'd been last night, he said frankly; he'd gone to a party and there'd been some high-grade grass and a few other things, and everybody must have had a good time and moved on, because the party had started at Doris's but when he woke up he was at Roberto's.

Whoever had pulled the heist last night hadn't been stoned, so they let him go. They were both feeling a little tired then so they sat there for a while smoking before they started looking for Rolando Garcia, and they were still there when the new call went down and Lake buzzed them.

"It's a body, at Seventh and Hill."

"My God, am I having a premonition?" said Palliser.

At that very busy corner, right in front of Bullocks' department store that ran through from Seventh to Eighth, of course there was a crowd. With the realization that something had happened or was happening, a lot of people tended to crowd up just to gawk, and the Traffic man first on the scene had evidently had to call a backup to make some effort at preserving order. There were three uniformed men standing spaced out behind one of the benches at the corner, and a fourth was standing in the street in front of it. Standing beside him was a civilian who was talking excitedly. And the body, slumped sideways on the bench, with quite a lot of blood all around it . . . "I knew it!" said Palliser savagely as they came up. "God damn it—"

"But didn't I say he's getting nuttier? Of all the places to commit a murder . . ." This was one of the most crowded spots in downtown L.A., where pedestrians and buses and cars made a hodgepodge of the narrow sidewalks and streets. During the middle of the day, on weekdays, it was nearly wall-to-wall people.

The Traffic men greeted them with relief. "It's been a job just to keep people from coming up to poke at the corpse," said Gomez feelingly. "I'd say you want to take him in as soon as possible, or we'll have traffic stalled."

"The lab will want photographs, though it's a waste of time," said Palliser. "Not one goddamned lead on this joker—"

"Well, you're going to get a good one," said a cheerful voice. Palliser turned.

"This is Mr. Trotwood," said Gomez. "Your only witness, Sergeant. And you might offer him some heartfelt thanks, he's been a big damned help in keeping the people away."

"Have to preserve the scene," said Trotwood. "It's Carl Trotwood, Sergeant, and I was glad to help out. I'm too short to pass the physical, but I've kind of made a hobby of—you know—police work. Police business." He was, quite simply, delighted to have stumbled into this, to be meeting real-life detectives. He looked at Palliser and Grace almost with affection. "To think it was me just happened to sit next to that

156

guy! But see, Sergeant, I trained myself to have a good memory for faces—always thought, I ever happen to be a witness to something important, I want to be a reliable one. And I got a very good close look at this killer—you put me at a table with an artist and an Identikit, and I'll give you a photograph of him! And I'll tell you something else very funny." Mr. Trotwood was a short broad dark fellow about thirty-five, with a homely round face and a big nose.

"That's fine, Mr. Trotwood, and we're very grateful for the help you gave the officers," said Palliser. "But just let us look at what we've got here—we'll get back to you presently."

"Oh, sure, sure, anything you say."

Grace was on the mike in one squad, to get a lab truck out. The body was a medium-sized man around sixty, in ordinary sports clothes; he had thinning gray hair, a pair of rimless spectacles had fallen to the sidewalk, and this was a messier kill than the others, a lot more blood spilled. There was a large canvas bag full of library books propped up against the bench beside him; all the books had been checked out today at the main library, Palliser discovered while they waited for the lab men.

The lab truck came, with the morgue wagon behind it; Horder took a couple of pictures for the record and then searched the body and handed a billfold to Grace.

There were a driver's license, a couple of credit cards, sixteen dollars in bills. His name was Eric Gustafson, he'd been fifty-nine and lived at a Hollywood address.

After the morgue wagon left, the crowd began to drift away, and Palliser and Grace took Carl Trotwood back to Palliser's car and put him in the back seat.

"Say, you know, I'm sorry as hell a man got killed," he said. "But all my life I've been interested in police work, in crime, and this is the first time I've ever been mixed up with it for real. I don't mean to sound as if I'm happy somebody got killed, but—well, I'm glad to be able to help you. I can tell you just what he looked like." He laughed. "Kind of a bonus, get out of going to the dentist."

"Oh? You were on the way to the dentist?"

"That's right, had an appointment at two-thirty. You see, I work right here at Bullocks', I drive one of the delivery vans. And we live in Atwater but I never drive to work on account of the parking being so expensive down here, leave the car to my wife. I had an appointment to have my teeth cleaned, Dr. Wilhelm out on Beverly, so I took off about one-forty to come down and catch the bus. And that guy was already sitting there, only one on the bench. The bus—my bus—was due about one-fifty. I wasn't paying any attention to the guy, just sitting there. And then this other one came up. He came right around in front of the bench"—Trotwood gestured—"and those benches are pretty close to the curb, you know, he was standing in the street—and on account of what he said I looked at him. Lots of people going by, but I don't suppose anybody heard him but me. He said, you're the one killed her, I found you now—and he just pulled this knife out of his pocket and starts stabbing the guy"—the gesturing was graphic now—"back, forth, back, forth, like lightning— I'm on my feet, he's maybe five feet away from me, I yell something like what the hell you think you're doing, and he turns and runs—up toward the corner, around on Seventh— and I tried to chase him, but I kept running into people, and all the crowds—he's gone. I came back, there's already people milling around on account of the blood. God, the fools there are in this world. I couldn't do everything at once," said Trotwood apologetically. "There's a pay phone on the corner, I called in to headquarters, but I couldn't swear that some of those damn people didn't leave prints all over, only I don't suppose it matters because he took the knife with him, and I never saw him touch the bench."

"That's very good, Mr. Trotwood."

"Now you give me a session with one of your artists, Sergeant, and I'll give you a composite like a photograph. He was six feet even, a hundred and seventy, that streaky dark and light blond hair, light eyes, a kind of pointed narrow chin, clean shaven—tufty sort of eyebrows and thin lips. But the funniest damned thing is," said Trotwood, "I've seen a picture of that guy before. I know I have. It's clear in my mind —I've seen a real photograph of him."

"That's not very likely, Mr. Trotwood," said Grace tactfully. "Maybe he just reminded you of somebody—"

"No, no," said Trotwood obstinately, "I've seen a photograph of him—if I could just remember where, damn it! But you give me a session with your Identikit."

At the address on Russell Street in Hollywood, the nice-looking brown-haired woman said blankly, before she broke down, "He always goes to the library once a week—he's a greater reader, he likes Westerns—and the car was on the fritz, he took the bus today— What? Why, he's the night security guard at the Universal Studio—you can't be telling me that Eric's *dead*—he's only fifty-nine—"

There was a son in West Hollywood to call, and a married daughter in La Habra.

Hackett and Landers had finally been able to get to some legwork, covering those various restaurants suggested to Upchurch by Seton, when the places began to open. They were all high-class, expensive restaurants; Landers snorted at Upchurch and his French cuisine. Upchurch so politically identified with those simple ranchers up north. They had started out at La Bella Fontana at the Beverly Wilshire Hotel, but everybody there shook their heads at the picture and said he hadn't been in there.

"It's possible," said Hackett, looking at the list, "that he stayed right where he was, Tom. At the Beverly Hilton. The big restaurant there is French—L'Escoffier. What the hell's that mean?"

"No idea," said Landers. "I took German."

"It's one of the places Seton said he recommended. And if Upchurch wasn't familiar with L.A. he might not have been inclined to go hunting for addresses. He wasn't far from his own hotel at the Hilton."

So they had come up here, to the dining room of L'Escoffier, opening at four. They showed the picture around, and the maître d' and all the waitresses shook their heads at it. He hadn't been there. They had, of course, seen the newspaper stories and pictures; they would have remembered.

"Well, the next nearest," said Hackett, "is this Jimmy's farther up in Beverly Hills."

But as they went through the lobby, they spotted Seton striding toward the front entrance, and Hackett increased his pace and caught up to him. "Afternoon, Mr. Seton. I should have picked up the nuances—that copy of *Playboy*—and of course you would have too. He had the roving eye, didn't he? He picked up a girl at the hotel as soon as he landed here, or did he have a date already set up? Was that just a call girl, or would you know?"

Seton met his eyes and gave a massive shrug. "So you're onto him. My God, Sergeant, that is the kind of thing we're paid to deal with—but if he was going to be that kind of a fool, I couldn't play nursemaid to him twenty-four hours a day. Yeah, I found out soon enough after we started dealing with him, he had quite an eye for the chicks, and I'd warned him to be discreet, for God's sake." Seton ran a hand over his smooth hair. "He was a good property," he said. "He put up such a damned good appearance, a slick actor, all those hicks up there eating out of his hand, and it was such a damned good image, the city folk liked him too." He looked reminiscent and thoughtful, his cold eyes introspective. "Why, hell, he could really have gone places, that one, it's a goddamned waste when you think of it—"

Hackett said, "It didn't cross your mind what harm a man like that might do the nation—a lecher, a man of no principle, susceptible to blackmail?"

Seton gave him a mirthless smile. "Sergeant, I'm a P.R. man. We get paid to build the image. What the hell, it was no skin off my nose."

Landers said very softly, "It will be, if we fall into a dictatorship on account of the corrupt politicians."

Seton shrugged again. "So you're one of the wild-eyed extremists. Common sense, boys. But Upchurch is a dead issue anyway, no use to anybody now. Forget it. And I've got an appointment with a client, excuse me." He turned to the door.

"Remind me to ask John," said Landers, "for a copy of that quote from Belloc."

EIGHT

Palliser and Grace were still out on the new call, whatever that was, on Tuesday afternoon when the autopsy report on Edna Patterson came in. Mendoza skimmed over it and said to Higgins, "Nothing we couldn't have guessed." She had been manually strangled. And she had been a medium-sized woman in reasonably good health, but if a big man had got her by the throat she wouldn't have had much chance to fight back.

When the new call came in at four-thirty, they both went out on it. "Getting along toward summer," said Higgins. "We'll be having a heat wave before long, and then see business really pick up."

It was a public high school on Forty-second Place, and as Higgins pulled into the parking lot the ambulance came out of it screaming. In the middle of the parking lot were a lot of excited adults and a handful of teen-agers and the two Traffic men, Faye and Corbett. They had sorted out the main facts, and presented them in capsule form.

"The supervisor of the cafeteria here, a Mrs. Joan Flowers, and one of the teachers, Arthur Robillard—he looked pretty bad. Two other cafeteria workers and a couple of kids saw it happen, everybody else came out afterward. This guy accosted Flowers as she was getting into her car, and Robillard evidently saw it and came running over to grab him—good many people leaving at this hour—and they were both shot. Senseless damned thing," said Faye. "Evidently he was after the money bag."

"What money bag?" asked Higgins.

"She always took the money from the cafeteria to deposit it at the bank. It's still in her car."

They talked to the two women, who also worked in the cafeteria, who had seen it happen: Mrs. Mona Knight, Miss Frances Medina. "We were just going along talking, coming to our cars, when I heard Mr. Robillard shout—he'd been just ahead of us—and I looked up, and he was running, and there were all of these loud bangs like firecrackers and this man beside Mrs. Flowers' car—"

"He was shooting at them, oh, it was awful, he'd already shot Mrs. Flowers, she was on the ground—"

"And then he just ran out of the lot."

Robillard was one of the teachers. There were eight other teachers there, but they had all come out on hearing the shots, hadn't seen anything.

One of the kids spoke up, a gangling black kid about sixteen. "I saw him pretty good, I was just behind them two"— he indicated the cafeteria workers—"and he looked a lot like Tommy."

Another one said jeeringly, "Man, don't tell the fuzz nothing no time," and surprisingly another couple of kids, one black and one probably Mexican, rounded on him.

"Bastard try to kill Mr. Robillard, I sure hope they get him—" "I tell the fuzz what I seen, that guy shoot Mr. Robillard—" Another four or five just stood watching, silent.

"All right," said Mendoza to the first one. "What's your name?"

"Derek Hornbuckle."

"So what did you see?"

"Lady from the cafeteria goin' up to her car—I was cuttin' through the lot on my way home after baseball practice. She put the money bag in the front seat, and then that guy came up from out back o' the car and point a gun at her. He looked an awful lot like that Tommy guy—he was a senior last year, I dint know him but he was a sorta big guy around account he was so good on the basketball team."

"Tommy Hernandez?" said one of the teachers. "Oh, it wouldn't have been Tommy—never any discipline problems, and a good background—really, Officers—"

"And then what?" asked Higgins.

"Mr. Robillard, he was just gettin' in his car and he seen him too, he yelled and started to run over there, and the guy shot at him and then he run across the lot and into the street. He hadn't no call to shoot Mr. Robillard!" said Derek shrilly. "I bet he was gonna steal the cafeteria money."

The teachers all said Robillard was one of the most popular teachers at the school; he taught shop and auto mechanics. Several of them said the Hornbuckle kid was imagining things, Tommy Hernandez had been one of their more docile pupils. "So," said Higgins to Derek, "just tell us what the fellow looked like—how tall, how old and so on."

"I dunno," said Derek, inarticulate. "Kind of old—uh, maybe twenny. Kind of tall, like Tommy. He had on a red shirt and dark pants. He run across the lot into the street, he put the gun back in his pocket."

Mendoza was talking to the two women, explaining that they would want statements. "A description," said Miss Medina. "Oh, dear, I couldn't—it was all so fast, I saw him running—oh, dear, it was so awful, poor Mrs. Flowers—all the blood—"

"He was pretty tall, and thin, all I could say," said Mrs. Knight. "Oh, my heavens, I hope they're both all right! Oh, somebody ought to call Mr. Krepps, the principal. Where should we call to find out about them?"

There probably wouldn't be a good description to get from any of them; it was just a senseless random thing. Mendoza

164

and Higgins went back to the office; tomorrow would be soon enough to write the initial report. Mendoza phoned the hospital. Robillard had been D.O.A., a bullet through the heart. Mrs. Flowers had a superficial shoulder wound and was in mild shock. "Well, small favors," said Mendoza. "She may have gotten a closer look at him. Maybe the night watch can talk to her."

He took the stodgy loaner back to the garage and picked up the Ferrari. When he turned up Hamlin Place, the last residential street in the city of Burbank, and on up the hill, he wondered about the gadget. When he came to the wrought-iron gates of La Casa de la Gente Feliz, he stopped and activated the gadget, and the gates obediently swung politely open and he drove through, watching the rear-view mirror; in thirty seconds they swung smartly closed with a little clang. Continuing on up the hill, he reflected that money was a useful commodity to possess, and it was also pleasant to live in an era where there were so many mechanical marvels available. At the garage, he pulled down the door on the Ferrari, Alison's Facel-Vega and Mairí's old Chevy. Kearney had installed a powerful floodlight on the garage roof, shining up the path to the back door. He came into the kitchen to find Mairí just taking a pot roast from the oven, Alison making a salad, and Cedric loudly slurping water from his bowl on the service porch.

"Hello, *querido.* Reasonably good day?"

And the twins came running. "Daddy, we been helpin' Uncle Ken build a fence—" "An' Terry almost got her finger nailed to the fence when she—"

El Señor appeared as if by conjuration when the cupboard was opened on the bottle of rye.

And Alison said, as they sat down to dinner, "They can't come to put up the block wall for nearly a month, and that wire-and-post thing looks absolutely horrible, but never mind —it'll get built eventually. And I just hope to goodness nothing else happens for a while!"

* * *

Schenke called the hospital, and was informed that Mrs. Flowers was still in shock and couldn't be talked to until tomorrow. The day men had left this list of possible suspects, and he and Piggott went out looking for a couple of those, leaving Conway to hold the fort. At nine-forty he got a call to a heist, a liquor store out at Sunset and Figueroa, and went out resignedly to listen to the same monotonous story: he had a gun, he said give me the money, I couldn't give you a description—

It was in a little triangle of business there, just below where the Hollywood freeway crossed the Pasadena freeway. The owner was a stolid beefily built man named Dunne. He said, "They came in here about half an hour ago, both black, one short fat guy, one tall skinny guy. They was waving guns around, and the tall one said let's have all the money, man. Now I never keep more than fifty bucks in the register, and I'd guess they got a little under that. So out they go, and I called in—"

"Them again," said Conway.

"You know 'em?"

"We do. Maybe sometime we'll drop on them."

"Well, I figure you have," said Dunne. "Time I finished calling, I heard an old engine grinding away, like the battery's down, and wondered if it was them, thought I'd try for a look at the plate number if it was—so I went out and spotted them, I'm pretty sure it was them, in an old white heap across the street. Only before I could get a look at the plate, it came to life and they took off, screeching rubber." He jerked his head. "Up there. I saw it, couldn't do anything to stop it. They hit the exit ramp of the Hollywood freeway doing about forty-five—God, a dozen signs, wrong way, do not enter—and the next minute, God, you shoulda heard the crash. So I called the Highway Patrol and I guess they're still up there clearing it all up. I'll bet it was a mess."

"For God's sake," said Conway. It was one way of clearing a case. He went up there; there was a police barrier across the exit, and a lot of jammed traffic was piled up. He climbed over the barrier, found a couple of Highway Patrol men named Unkovitch and Twelvetrees, and explained.

"Christ," said Unkovitch, "the damn fools we have to deal with! Look at it." The wreckage was impressive. The Ford, headed straight for oncoming traffic, had hit head on with a brand new Honda Civic, though you couldn't tell what it had been now; everybody in both those cars was dead. Behind the Honda, a Buick had plowed into the first two, and behind that five other cars had slewed around and barged into each other and the central divider, trying to avoid the tangled wreck. "Nine people in the hospital and four dead," said Unkovitch. "The people in the Honda were just a young couple, John and Ruth Rudd, address in Bel Air. There was a number to call in emergency, I just got back from doing it. The guy went to pieces. She was expecting a baby."

"God," said Conway. "What about the Ford? You get any I.D.?"

"I don't know why the hell I picked this job," said Twelvetrees. "Poking around in blood and brain tissue. There was a driver's license issued in Missouri for a Roy Johnson, the car had Missouri plates. Also a traffic ticket, written up yesterday, for an illegal left downtown, and it's got an address on Sixty-second on it. We don't know who the other man was, and nobody's going to identify him by what's left of his face."

"We can probably find out," said Conway. "We'll take care of that one." He took down the address. He went back to the office and found Schenke there, and they went out together to Sixty-second Place.

It was a crumbling old apartment building, and there was a handwritten slip saying *Johnson* in the mail slot of apartment twelve. There they found a couple of women, and broke the news. It seemed that the other one had been Elmer Johnson, and they were cousins.

"Never wanted to come all the way out here, he was the one—say do better out here, down on our luck like we been—"

"But it sure hasn't been no better out here, and what we gonna do now, Della?"

"I don't reckon we got the bread to get home on—"

"Let alone pay for no funeral—"

When they got back to the office, Piggott told them that the man with the Doberman had been out again. "Couple named Kahn, they'd been to a big revue of some kind at the Shrine Auditorium. Came out to the parking lot late, and he walked up to them from the street. He got about forty dollars."

"Oh, for God's sake," said Schenke. "That is about the craziest we've had in a while."

"Let's hope the idea doesn't catch on," said Conway. "We'll have a committee getting under way to outlaw all Dobermans."

Hackett and Landers were doing the overtime, necessarily, covering those restaurants. They had started out at Chez Claude, gone on to François's, and drawn a blank; they had tried Jimmy's. They had gone back to the Beverly Wilshire Hotel to check a little bar they had missed there before. Everywhere people had looked at the picture and said no. And said, this was the guy in all the papers, wasn't it, and they'd have remembered.

They stopped for dinner at a middle-class place in West Hollywood, and being technically off duty had a drink beforehand. Nine o'clock found them at the Century-Plaza Hotel in Century City.

That particular enormous new hotel and shopping complex had several restaurants, banquet rooms, all sorts of shops in several directions off the main lobby, and there were three levels of halls and restaurants under the main lobby. The Granada was down on the lowest level; they took the escalator, Landers complaining that it made him nervous. "I don't mind the damn things going up, but coming down—"

The maître d' at the Granada and six waiters looked at

the picture and said no. The gentleman had never been here. It was the gentleman in the papers, yes, well, they would have remembered.

"Well, that's that," said Landers. "Where the hell did he go? Now we know it wasn't any of these Seton recommended, my God, there are a million restaurants in this town."

They started out, past the big double doors, and Hackett said, "There's no way to know, damn it. But the press, Tom— don't you think, if any maître d' or waiter anywhere had seen him somewhere Saturday night, they'd have come forward and said so? I don't know what that might say. Wait a minute. Wait a minute." He stopped. "But we are a couple of damned fools, Tom."

"How come?"

"The autopsy report, God damn it! A couple of scotch highballs. He didn't have dinner on Saturday night."

"Good God, of course not. We should have—"

"All right," said Hackett. "Think about it. Drinks. A bar. And here's a place where we haven't asked." It was the little separate bar attached to the Granada, just outside the entrance and angled off to one side.

"Well, why not?" said Landers. "Last throw of the dice."

They went in. It wasn't very big, perhaps forty by thirty feet, and unlike most of its kind it was fairly well lighted. There was a small bar at the far end, little octagonal tables and barrel chairs upholstered in red vinyl. At this hour there was only one couple there, intimate over drinks at a table near the door, and the bartender leaning meditatively on the bar.

They went up and sat on a couple of backless stools. "Do for you?" asked the bartender.

Hackett got out one of the leaflets, and showed him the badge. "Did you see this man in here on Saturday night?"

The bartender took it and studied the photograph. He was a brawny big man somewhere in the forties, with a tough gangsterish face slightly scarred by old acne, and black hair.

They thought he wasn't going to answer, but after a long time he said argumentatively, "Damn it, this *was* the guy. I said it was."

"In here?" asked Hackett. "Saturday night?"

"Said it to who?" asked Landers.

"I said it to my wife, and she said don't be silly, Kev— excuse me, gents, I'm Kevin Houlihan—she says don't be silly, it couldn't be because the paper said he was such a steady family man and a churchgoer and all that, so I shut up. But damn it, now I see this, by God it *was* him. I'd swear to it."

"Here, Saturday night? When?"

"Well, I'll tell you all about it, you interested," said Houlihan. "God, I'll bet that dame had a fit when he dropped dead of the heart attack or whatever it was. Funny how things happen. But I'll take my oath it *was* that guy. It was about a quarter past six Saturday night, and there wasn't hardly any customers in. See, a lot of people go right in the restaurant and have drinks at the table, it's only when they got no reservations and have to wait, or want to kill some time, they come in here. There were only a couple of men in, seemed to be talking business. And the blonde. And then this guy comes in, and he orders a scotch highball, and he sits here and drinks some of it, and then he goes over and picks up the blonde."

Landers laughed. "That's our boy. We might have known. As easy as that?"

"Well, I figure she was kind of ripe for the picking," said Houlihan, with a meditative grin. "She'd been sitting there getting madder and madder—she'd been here since about five-fifteen, and she wasn't covering up either—it was pretty damn obvious some guy had stood her up. She'd been lookin' at her watch every three minutes, and tapping her fingers on the table, and looking up at the door whenever anybody passed, you know the routine."

"You ever see her before?" asked Landers.

"Not in here, but I'd seen her before. Just that afternoon, upstairs in the Garden Room when I was coming on duty.

170

That was just before four, we open here at four. The hotel puts on all sorts of fancy doings, you know, and there was some kind of fashion show going on in there, dames parading around to show off clothes, and she was one of them, she was down by the door to the lobby when I came past. I noticed her because, gents, she'd stand out in any crowd, silver-blond hair kind of long and wavy, and pretty tall, and more figure than those skinny models usually have."

"You sure?" asked Hackett.

"I'm sure. I recognized her when she came in, even if she had different clothes on. She'd sat here from about five-fifteen on, getting madder and madder after it got past six o'clock. She had two daiquiris, made them last, and I was just wondering if she was going to order a third one when this guy walked over and annexed her."

"And then what happened?"

"Well, they talked, and he had another highball and bought her another daiquiri. She started looking a lot happier—well, he was a good-lookin' guy, wasn't he?—looked as if he was loaded, too—and about seven-fifteen they got up and went out together. And that's the last I saw of 'em. But damn it, I'm positive it was this guy."

"It was him," said Landers. "Running true to form."

"And it should be fairly easy to locate the girl," said Hackett. "That's all very helpful, Mr. Houlihan, thanks very much."

"Can I quote you?" asked Houlihan.

"What?"

"To my wife. You think it was him too, hah? Good. It's not very often I can get the police to back me up in an argument."

"I don't know if you'll see it in the papers," said Landers, "but you can quote us."

They went upstairs to the main desk. "Well, all that sort of thing is arranged by our social activities director," explained the desk clerk. "I don't know whether she'd be on the premises at this hour, but there is that crafts display being set up in the Hawaiian Room, I can check—"

The social activities director was Miss Suzanne Winter, sleek and dark, and she said at once that all the models and clothes for the fashion show had come from Genevieve Du Mond in Beverly Hills.

On Wednesday morning, with Higgins off, Mendoza digested that and said, "However he died, I'm just as happy he won't be on the June ballot."

"Yes, damn it, but all that doesn't suggest what did happen to him," said Landers.

"He could have just gotten drunk and fallen down," said Hackett. "Bainbridge said it could have happened that way. And the blonde was scared and cleared out."

"They were sitting necking in the parking lot of the County Courthouse?" said Mendoza.

Landers grinned. "Well, you've got to admit it's a nice quiet private place at night."

"Well, you should locate her without much trouble. It'll be interesting to hear what she has to say."

"And I suppose the fancy high-fashion place doesn't open until ten o'clock or so. It's out on Sunset, I looked it up."

Palliser, Grace and Glasser had been listening to that. They had, of course, heard all about the Johnsons from Conway's report overnight; one less to work, and good riddance. Palliser started to say something about politicians, and Lake came in with a manila folder and handed it to Grace. "Slow but sure," said Grace. "At last, the lab report on the Patterson house."

"Anything in it?" asked Palliser.

"Let's see." Grace began to read, and two minutes later said pleasedly, "Now isn't that nice. They picked up quite a few good latents all over the place, which don't belong to the family, and they've found some in our records, and they belong to a burglar by the name of Dwight Goodis. Now where the hell have I heard that name before? Where— My God, it's the name of that lowlife couple who live right across the street—but I don't think the wife called him Dwight.

And there's a different address here—he's on parole, so they'll know downstairs." He picked up the phone and asked Lake to get him the Welfare and Rehab office.

Goodis's parole officer was a fellow named Roth. He said, "That's the right address, Van Ness. He's only been out for four months, don't tell me he's been up to something else. Well, I got him a pretty good job with a furniture company, Eagle Rattan Imports, but he's fairly stupid, I don't know how long he'll keep it."

"Did you say a furniture company?" asked Grace.

"That's right. He's driving a delivery van for them."

"Oh, thank you so much," said Grace. He passed that on and Mendoza began to laugh.

"If they weren't so stupid we wouldn't pick up as many as we do, Jase. Go get him and we'll hear what he has to say."

Glasser and Wanda had gone to the hospital to talk to Mrs. Flowers. Palliser drove down to the address on Van Ness, while Grace looked up the furniture store to go and collar Goodis. The place on Van Ness was another old apartment; the Goodises lived upstairs at the back. When a sharp-featured medium-brown young woman opened the door, he could see past her, just at one glance, several items that looked like some on the list Linda Gilman had given them.

"What you want, bust in here like— Oh." She looked at the badge.

"Come on, Mrs. Goodis. You're coming in to talk to us."

"What about? We haven't done nothing. You damn cops can't—"

"Oh, yes, we can. With you displaying Edna Patterson's furniture all over your living room. But more important than that, your husband left us some nice fingerprints in that house."

"Oh, my God!" she said disgustedly. "Oh, that damn stupid lousy nigger, if I told him once I told him a million times—" Most of the way back to the office she told Palliser, in various colorful language, just how stupid that no-good Dwight was and how stupid she'd been to marry him.

Ten minutes after Palliser brought her in, Grace came back with Dwight Goodis. He was a great big burly black man in the early twenties, still looking surprised and aggrieved to have been dropped on. As soon as she saw him she screamed, "Goddamn stupid bastard! Leavin' prints all over that damn place!"

An interrogation room was too small for them both; they sat them down in the communal office and Mendoza came out to sit in. "Now, now," said Grace benevolently, "let's not have any of that. Now you know we've got the solid evidence on you, Dwight, suppose you tell us all about the job."

"Damn fingerprints," he said.

"Oh, you make me sick, you dumb bastard. I told you and told you—"

"Let's hear about it," said Palliser. "Just why did you have to kill Mrs. Patterson?"

"Well, God damn it," said Goodis sullenly, "she wasn't supposed to be there—how'd I know she was gonna be there? Eddy said she always went to church Wednesday night, didn't get home till late. I was gonna bring the van, load everything—"

"You were just after the furniture?" asked Grace incredulously.

"Yeah, yeah, that's right. Nice furniture, Eddy said. See, him an' Josie just moved into that place across the street, an' he said he took a letter over to her once, got left their place by mistake, an' saw she hadda lotta real nice stuff. We was just talkin', see, because me and Lois didn't have no furniture atall, and we hadda move outta that place on Fifty-sixth because it's gonna be torn down, that place was all furnished, and damn it, all we could find for any kinda decent rent we could pay was the place on Van Ness and there wasn't nothin' in it atall. And my God, any o' that stuff so high now, nobody could hardly afford to buy it, and we ain't got good credit . . ." He was explaining earnestly just how justified the job had been. "And Eddy said why don't I get the van and take some of her stuff while she's at church, it'd be easy as pie—I got the key of the company's garage and the van, see. I just parked it in the drive while everybody along there'd prob'ly be havin' dinner—"

"My God," said Grace suddenly, "we never asked the neighbors about Wednesday night—those upstanding respectable neighbors—I'll bet a lot of them were at church too."

"Yeah, yeah, that's what Eddy said, people on both sides be out too—and we went up to the back door and it wasn't even locked—"

"We, who was with you?"

"Well, Lois, acourse. And Eddy, help move the stuff. Only, God damn it, the old lady was there! She come into the kitchen in a bathrobe, she lets out a yip, and I could see she was goin' to scream an' yell, and I just grabbed her to keep her quiet. I never meant to kill her."

"And as long as you're stupid enough to let them drop on you, take everybody else to the joint with you!" She looked at the detectives. "There was a hell of a lot of nice stuff there, when I seen how good it was I said, think about the family, most of them needed a lot of things, the welfare only goes so far, you know. And I called up Pete and Joey and Benny and Gene—they're his cousins—and my brother Bill, and they all come and helped load the van. We had a hell of a time, get everything on, but we did it, and just about in time too. We was just comin' up to the corner, starting away, when a car passed us and turned in the drive right next to that place. The rest of 'em had just about got back to their cars. We spent the rest o' the night delivering all the stuff, but I took my pick first. Everybody needed things, better mattresses an' chairs an' tables an' all."

"My God," said Grace, awed. And what a job this was going to be, sorting out where all that had gotten to; and they would all share in the charge; at least Eddy would share the homicide charge, the job had evidently been largely his idea.

"So let's have some names and addresses," said Mendoza briskly.

She began to rattle them off, and Grace took notes. Now they'd be busy the rest of the day bringing them all in, talking to them, getting statements. And looking for the furniture—and that was going to clutter up a lot of evidence space downstairs until the case was disposed of—at least until the statements were on file and the D.A. had the case outlined, when the family could have it back.

Palliser had gone to apply for the warrants.

Mrs. Joan Flowers looked up at them from her hospital bed, and her eyes were filled with tears. She wasn't much hurt, and would probably be released tomorrow. She was a fat, placid-faced woman in her fifties. She said, "The most awful thing about it is Mr. Robillard getting killed. They only told me last night. That's just an awful thing. Everybody liked him so much, and he was so good with the boys—I've heard more than one teacher say that he'd saved a lot of boys from going to the bad, getting them interested in a trade. I sort of feel like I'd killed him myself."

"We'd like to find out who did it," said Glasser. "What do you remember? Can you give us a description of him?"

"I only saw him for a flash—before he shot me, you know. I'd just put the bag of money in the front of my car—"

"How much would there have been in it?"

"Well, it's a big school, and it's scandalous how—even down there—the kids always seem to have money. A lot of mothers too lazy to bother fixing a lunch. A lot of the kids eat at the cafeteria. I suppose there'd be between four and five hundred dollars."

"All right, he came from behind your car and pointed the gun at you. Think back. What did he look like?"

"He was kind of tall," she said slowly. "Kind of thin. He was a white fellow, but dark-skinned—not very old, I guess."

"Somebody told us he thought it looked like a kid named Tommy Hernandez. Do you know him? He was in school last year."

She shook her head. "I don't know any of the kids. They're

just faces. I'm back in the kitchens mostly, supervising the cooking."

They drove down to the school and saw the principal, listened to a lot of platitudes and asked about Hernandez. "Oh, yes, he was quite a star on the basketball team last year. Mr. Wrangell was telling me that one of the students there yesterday said the killer looked like him. Ridiculous. What? Well, I haven't any idea where Hernandez is now. He graduated in February, and his address won't be in our files now."

Hackett and Landers landed at Genevieve Du Mond in Beverly Hills at its opening hour, ten-thirty. It could scarcely be called a shop: the first room beyond the elegant black and gold front door was furnished as a rather bare living room, with a white-velvet couch and chairs, a gilt-framed mirror on one wall; an archway showed them a larger room up a few steps, lined with plate-glass mirrors. There was no sign of any female clothes at all.

Genevieve turned out to be, when she looked at the badge in Hackett's hand, Mrs. Marlene Bloom. She was dark and rather gaunt, with cynical shrewd eyes; and she looked nonplussed at two detectives in her establishment—it could only be called that. But she looked at Hackett's height and bulk with veiled admiration, at Landers' lank dark boyishness with a quick smile.

"And just what's behind the questions about that do at the hotel? Somebody lose a purse or a mink stole?"

"Nothing like that," said Hackett. "It's nothing to do with you at all, I don't think. What about the models you use? Where do they come from?"

"The girls? Well, when I'm putting on a show as big as that, I have to hire extra. I always use Lowrie's agency. I had five extra girls that day. I employ three of my own, to model for clients."

"We're interested in one who was there Saturday. She's described as tall, with silver-blond hair and a very good figure."

"Rosalie Packard," she said instantly. "She's one of my girls —and a good girl, a nice girl. What do you think Rosalie's done?"

"We have to talk to her," said Hackett. "Is she here now?"

She was studying them. "I don't like this. She's a nice girl."

"She may be, but we have to talk to her. Is she?"

"No. She's not due in until one. Well, I suppose I can't hold out on the police, and you'd find her anyway." She plucked one of her cards from the pretty gilt container on a table and held out her hand; Hackett gave her a ballpoint pen and she scribbled on the card. "I hope you're not going to arrest her. She's going to be a very good model—still getting experience, but she's quick to learn."

"And thanks so much," said Hackett. "Now tell us something else. That fashion show on Saturday. How did the girls get there?"

"Well, the Lowrie girls provide their own transportation, but I took my girls, and all the models to be displayed. I've got a station wagon."

"So Rosalie rode out to the Century-Plaza with you. But she didn't come back with you, did she?"

"Well, well, aren't you the smart detective, Sergeant. How did you know that? No, she had a date later, she said her boy friend was picking her up there after the show."

Outside, Hackett looked at the card. "Selma Avenue, that's just above the Strip. I think Luis'd like to sit in on this, let's pick him up on the way."

When they dropped into the office, everything was humming at top speed; everybody was going to be busy on the Patterson thing for a while to come, with so many people involved. They collected Mendoza and went out to Hackett's Monte Carlo again and started for Hollywood.

The Sunset Strip, these days, was looking a little tawdry and tired, in spite of a couple of newish high-rise office buildings. The residential areas above Sunset, once fashionable addresses, had aged into middle-class dreariness. Rosalie Packard lived in an upstairs apartment in an eight-unit building at the top of Selma Avenue; its square stucco design made it look stodgy and respectable.

They climbed steep stairs, found the door; Landers pushed the bell. In thirty seconds the door opened, and there she was. They could see why the bartender had remembered her. She was a very striking-looking piece of goods indeed; long wavy silver-gilt hair, a lovely oval face with arched brows, a beautifully cut mouth, very large blue eyes, and a figure to draw whistles a block away. She was wrapped in a lime-green terry robe, and she stared at the three men on her doorstep and went deathly pale.

"Police, Miss Packard," said Mendoza briskly. "I don't think we need to tell you what it's about."

She was scared to death; she stepped back as she might have from a snake in the path, and she began to cry a little, the tears welling up and rolling down slowly. "Oh—oh—oh!" she said. "Oh, it was all so silly—I never meant anything and Stan never meant anything, it just *happened*—it wasn't any-body's fault but you're not going to believe it—oh—oh—oh!"

"Suppose you try us," said Landers.

She just sat down on the couch and looked at them as if she expected them to produce the handcuffs any minute. "I was—just so mad—at Stan"—her mouth was trembling and her voice shook—"and he flies into such a temper at any-thing—and—it—all—just—happened—"

The apartment was brightly and smartly furnished, and looked unexpectedly homey; it was very neat and clean. There were, unexpectedly, family photographs scattered around: a couple of younger girls enough like her to be sisters, a hand-some middle-aged couple, even what looked like a possible grandmother.

"And—oh—oh—it was bad enough, it was awful, what happened, but when it was in all the papers—*who he was*— and all the fuss on TV—*oh, my heavens*, I've never been so scared in my life! I told Stan you'd find out—oh, oh, oh— and he said no way, don't worry—but I did, and now you have, and you'll say it was murder and put us both in jail

179

and I'll just *die of shame*—never could look Mother in the face again, she was so dead set against my coming to Hollywood in the first place—she'll say—she'll say—I was tempted of the devil—and it was all just an accident, but I knew you'd find out—oh, oh, oh—"

"Stan who?" asked Mendoza.

She gulped. "Stan P-P-Powell."

"And where do we find him?"

She was weeping in earnest now, "Wh-Whaley and Dunlop —Architects. Sh-Sherman Oaks."

Stan Powell was big and burly, with shoulders like a prize-fighter's and sandy-red hair. He sat in the chair beside Mendoza's desk and said candidly, "Hell, hell, hell. My God, I'm just sorry Rosalie's involved in this damned thing, but then it wouldn't have happened without Rosalie. I know I've got hell's own temper, it goes off like a bomb."

"It was my fault too," she choked. "Let him pick me up— like a cheap tart—but he was polite—"

"Oh, for God's sake!" said Powell. He was only about twenty-six; they'd heard by now that she was twenty-two. "I had a date to meet Rosalie there—she had this fashion show bit there, and it'd be just as convenient to pick her up there. Five-thirty to six, I said. Only I got hung up on the freeway. I'd been out in Tarzana at the site of a new shopping center we're designing, and I was on the Ventura Freeway, there was a big semi had turned over and traffic was piled up for miles. I was stuck, no way to get off. I just had to sit there until they finally got one lane clear, and I never got to the Century-Plaza till after seven o'clock." He was talking bluntly, roughly, and that would be his natural manner: an almost aggressively honest young man. "I pulled into the public hotel lot behind, the one where you don't have to pay, and just as I turned up one aisle looking for a slot, I saw Rosalie getting in a car with this fellow—couldn't miss her hair in the arc light—"

"Oh, it was all my fault—if I hadn't—"

"And, God, I just lost my temper—we're practically engaged, she should have known I had some good reason for being late, but she's got a temper too—"

"I was—so mad—at you, and he was pretty smooth, made me laugh—"

"It was too late to get at them there, he was backing out, so I took off after them, and when he got onto Olympic I knew where they were heading—same place we'd been going to, she's crazy about the damn fool place, Madame Nu's in Little Tokyo. He pulled in the lot, found a slot and drove in, and I just slammed out of my car and caught them as they got out. I said something like what the hell you think you're doing with my girl, and he started to say something but I didn't listen, I hit him and I connected all right, but—" Powell lifted his shoulders in a massive shrug and planted both hands on his knees: they were square capable artist's hands. "I'm no boxer, I got him on the shoulder and he was off balance and fell back against the car, and Rosalie let out a yelp and—well, he didn't get up. My God. I didn't believe it but he was unconscious, he'd knocked himself out. Rosalie was in a dither, but I said no sweat, put him in the car and leave him somewhere, when he wakes up maybe he'll think twice about stealing another man's girl—and maybe Rosalie'll think twice about stepping out on me again—"

"Why in God's name the County Courthouse?" asked Mendoza.

"Well, I didn't want to leave him right there, in case he came in the restaurant and started a scene. And just a few blocks up there was this empty lot—Rosalie was trailing me in my car—"

"I was shaking so bad I could hardly drive—"

"And I just left him. And—"

"Did you wipe your prints off the wheel?"

"Well, for God's sake, no—why should I? I thought he'd come to and be okay. We went back to the restaurant and, well, made up— And then, sweet Jesus, on Monday it came out who he was, and he was dead—I didn't believe it, I thought some hophead must have come along after we left and hit him on the head for his roll—could that have happened?" They shook their heads at him. "But what the papers said—my God, I never meant to kill anybody!"

"That's a very interesting little story, Mr. Powell," said Mendoza. "For what it's worth, I don't think you'll spend much time in jail. At an educated guess, the D.A.'s going to call it voluntary manslaughter, and you might get a suspended sentence." He looked at Rosalie paternally, across his steepled hands. "I don't think Miss Packard will be charged with anything, although she did—mmh—supply the provocation."

"Well, praise heaven for that!" said Powell. "Okay, chief, bring on the handcuffs, I'm ready. I hope the firm will take an open view about it, it's a good job."

Landers took him over to the jail. The warrant had been applied for, and he would probably make bail. Wanda said sympathetically that she'd drive Rosalie home.

"The only thing is, Luis," said Hackett, "the D.A. may want to make an example of him, and a judge might go along. Soft as be damned on the street punks hitting old ladies over the head, but the respectable citizen who kills an important politician deserves the full treatment."

"*Dios*, let's hope not, Art. If she cries like that on the stand, looking about three years old and begging Daddy to fix her doll, he won't get convicted of anything." He began to laugh again. "It's just what Alison says—another case of one thing leading to another!"

Bill Moss was riding a squad along Pico Boulevard about ten-thirty that night, when an old tan Buick ahead of him ran a light. There wasn't much traffic out and no harm was done, but examples had to be set and careless drivers warned. Moss speeded up a little and touched the siren, and half a block up the Buick pulled into an empty spot at the curb. Moss pulled up behind it.

He got out, automatically putting on his cap and feeling for the book of tickets in his pocket. And then, as he started up to the driver's side of the Buick, a cold finger went up his spine and he remembered the briefing at roll call the other day. All of them had been remembering that briefing whenever they pulled a car over lately. And the Buick was wearing out-of-state plates. Leroy Rogers' mug shot had been reproduced and passed around. He was around here somewhere, and he was trigger-happy.

The plates on the Buick were Texas. It could be just a tourist, and you didn't want to give them a bad image of California cops; he couldn't go up there with his gun out, for somebody running a red light.

Between two footsteps he thought of it all: the chances: and any possible compromise. He'd gotten shot up a while ago, and he didn't like hospitals; he probably wouldn't like a niche in the mausoleum any better.

He walked up to the driver's window and before he got there he sang out in a genial voice, "Sorry to pull you over, sir!"

He got there. He looked down at Leroy Rogers behind the wheel, big and blond and armed and dangerous, and he grinned at him as friendly as a yellow pup and he said, "I'm not about to give you a ticket, sir, but I just noticed your tail light's out, and I thought you ought to know."

"Oh," said Rogers. "Is it?"

"Yes, sir." Moss leaned easily on the car door. "It looks to me as if somebody's banged into you, your tail pipe's knocked sideways too, could be dangerous. Some of these public lots, with females trying to park—you know."

Rogers grinned back, displaying a fine set of white teeth. "Don't we know. Well, thanks."

"You'd better step out and take a look," said Moss. "That tail pipe's about ready to let go."

"For God's sake," said Rogers, "all I need, a repair bill." The southern accent was pronounced. He opened the door and got out. Moss looked for the Colt, didn't see any bulges. Rogers walked toward the rear of the car, and Moss said, "Okay, Rogers, hold it! Spread 'em! Hands on the car." He

183

poked the Police Positive into Rogers' back and brought out the cuffs.

Rogers was still telling him about his ancestry and habits, showing a colorful vocabulary, when Wray and Dunning came roaring up five minutes later. They found the Colt under the front seat of the Buick. Tomorrow, the front office would find out that the Buick had been stolen in Houston three weeks back.

NINE

On Thursday morning, with Hackett off, everybody was highly amused at the solution of the Upchurch case, and gratified at getting Leroy Rogers out of circulation. Everybody was also a little surprised at Higgins' reaction to Goodis and his pals: he cussed about that for five minutes until Grace said, "Just a gang of the usual stupid punks, George."

"Yes, I know," said Higgins, "but damn it, there was something about that got to me, Jase—that poor old woman. Anyway, we've got them, and what a hell of a job to clean up." He got on the phone to Atlanta about Rogers; Atlanta would have priority, and probably send somebody to escort him back there.

Palliser, Landers, Glasser and Grace went out to discover where all the Patterson furniture had ended up. For once, nothing new had happened overnight.

Mendoza told Lake to phone the local press; he'd give them an interview at ten o'clock about Upchurch.

Marx called from SID just before the press arrived. "The morgue sent over the slug from your new corpse. We picked up some ejected cartridge cases in that parking lot, so it came as no surprise. It's a thirty-two automatic, probably an old Colt. You ever pick it up, we can tie it in."

"*Gracias,*" said Mendoza. That was just up in the air, no leads at all, no kind of description.

When the press showed up, he gave them the bare facts on Upchurch, and they were very happy with the story. "Hot damn," said the *Times* man mildly, "another great leader shows feet of clay. It'll make a nice second subhead, Lieutenant, of course it'd rank real headlines if he'd already been elected."

"And everybody forget about it the next day," said the *Herald* sadly. "I suppose there's not a hope of getting at Powell for an interview, but the girl . . ." They went away to write their stories, and Mendoza reflected that they were going to be wild about Rosalie; he laid a private bet with himself that large pictures of Rosalie were going to appear in the papers, whether they paid much attention to Powell before the arraignment.

Lake came in and said there was a Mr. Chalfont asking to see him.

"Oh? Well, bring him in."

There entered a short stout dark man in an ill-fitting bright brown suit. He said, his eyes sliding away from Mendoza's, that he was Gregory Parmenter's lawyer. "I have been out of town, and I've just learned of his very regrettable death—not being able to contact him, I went to the pharmacy, and a Mr. Rauschman"—his prim mouth twitched disagreeably—"at the establishment next door informed me—"

"Oh, yes," said Mendoza. "What can we do for you, Mr. Chalfont?"

"The keys to the house. I believe the police must have them. And to the pharmacy. I am putting the will in probate, of course, and must have access."

Mendoza had forgotten the keys; the feds had handed them back, and he rummaged in the top drawer of the desk, found them and handed them over. "There was a will?" He was, for no reason, surprised. "May I ask you how it reads?"

"I expect you would be interested," said Chalfont grudgingly. "Everything is left to his only relative, a niece living in Colfax. Of course the first thing I must do is arrange a funeral. That will be extremely simple—Mr. Parmenter was an atheist, and would deplore any elaborate service."

And that was not at all surprising, considering what they knew about Parmenter. Mendoza sat back, after Chalfont had sidled out, and thought about Parmenter. He had said to Hackett, he supposed the only answer on Parmenter was one of the brotherhood, but how likely was that, really? He wondered if Chalfont was another member of the brotherhood, and decided that he probably was. What kind of quarrel could there have been between Parmenter and one of the brothers? Possibly Parmenter had ambitions toward taking over the local leadership—but when you thought about it, as Grady had said, men like that were unimportant men, failures in life, and not (like the real terrorists) men of action. They got their kicks out of producing the hate literature; could you see one like that actually taking the personal violent action?

Well, it was an academic question—Mendoza yawned and stretched—and he supposed he'd better do some work, help out on the Patterson thing; there was a lot of paperwork still to do.

By midafternoon, they had all the furniture spotted and being transported into the police garage, the only space for it temporarily. The family could come and identify it tomorrow, and then they could have it back; it couldn't be left to clutter up the place. This case was costing time and money. And, Grace pointed out, the city would have to pay the transport charges to get it back to the family, not their fault, they couldn't be stuck with the delivery charge.

Higgins and Landers had no sooner landed back at the office after lunch than they had to rush out again, to a body in a hotel room over on Temple. When Higgins came back to write the report, he said, "Another damned anonymous thing. That place isn't so much a hotel as a cheap rooming house, the clerk on the desk is more like a manager and rent collector. The roomers—ninety-five percent male—next door to being derelicts, picking up the part-time jobs—a scattering of oldsters on Social Security—some of them on the way down and out."

"I know the type. So?"

"So, this Thomas Fuller. He's been there about a month. Man around fifty, nondescript. Comes and goes, nobody knows if he has a job or what it is. He came in last night, says the clerk, about eight o'clock, with another man. He can't describe the other man. They were arguing about something, he thought, can't say about what. An hour and a half ago a tenant who lives down the hall came home, noticed Fuller's door open and him sprawled on the floor. He's been shot—somebody used the bed pillow to muffle the noise. I left the lab there and Tom trying to get some answers out of the other people at home."

"Bricks without straw," said Mendoza absently.

"You can say so. The room on one side of his is empty, but I want to talk to the fellow in the one on the other side, what's his name, Gillespie, but he isn't home. The clerk says sometimes he doesn't come back for a couple of days, doesn't know where he goes, but he's paid up so he probably will be back. See if he heard anything, or saw the man who came in with Fuller. My God, what a place." Higgins sorted out carbon, rolled the triplicate forms into his typewriter.

Palliser and Glasser came back to write the inevitable follow-up reports on the disposition of evidence in the Patterson case. Wanda was down at the D.A.'s office giving moral support to Rosalie Packard. The office was clinking along quietly at normal speed, about three o'clock, when a man came rushing in and said loudly to Lake, "Sergeant Palliser—I've got to see Sergeant Palliser! By God, they both thought I was crazy, but I found it! Is Sergeant Palliser here?"

Palliser went out to the corridor, and Carl Trotwood gave him a vast beaming grin. "I know you thought I was crazy, Sergeant—eager beaver amateur imagining things, hah? But

I knew I'd seen it—a photograph of that killer—and I got to wracking my brains, where the hell could it have been? Only one logical answer, I says to myself, and I've been looking—because I subscribe to all of 'em, all the true detective magazines, and I save 'em, I've got a big collection. I've been back through the last six months of issues, whenever I got time, ever since that happened. And just now, I'm on my coffee break at work, I pick up this one, and there he is, by God!" He thrust a magazine with a garish cover at Palliser; he had a slip of paper marking the page, and opened it and folded it back and jabbed his finger at it. "That's him, Sergeant—I'd swear it on a stack of Bibles—that's the guy who stabbed that fellow."

Palliser took one look and prodded Trotwood into Mendoza's office. They spread the magazine on Mendoza's desk and skimmed through the story hastily. The magazine was a four-month-old copy of *Master Detective*, and one of its features appearing every so often was "Do You Remember This Unsolved Case?" "That," said Trotwood triumphantly again, "is him." The full-page photograph on the left-hand side had been blown up from a much smaller candid shot, but it was clear enough: a nice-looking boy about nineteen or twenty, with an engaging grin, fair hair, a pointed chin, wide-set eyes.

Mendoza skimmed through the story, Palliser reading over his shoulder. Six years ago, two young college kids on a date, Don Holland and Jean Tuesche: students at Pasadena City College. They'd been parked in a lovers' lane above Altadena when a man drove up, put a gun on them, locked Holland in the trunk, drove off elsewhere, eventually raped and killed the girl and nearly killed Holland. They were found the next day up by Devil's Gate Dam. But Holland, evidently keeping his head and thinking coolly, had memorized the plate number of the killer's car. He had scrawled it on his shirt cuff while he was locked in the trunk, before the killer beat him up so badly he had to have brain surgery. The Pasadena police had run a make on it, and it belonged to a man named Floyd Seacarn.

They found the car abandoned in a lot on Third Street in L.A., and they traced Seacarn to a nearby hotel, where he'd been registered for four days. Holland had given them a description: a medium-sized man about fifty-five, brown hair, glasses. Seacarn had a record in San Francisco and Fresno of rape, attempted rape, assault with violence; he'd just been released from Susanville where he'd been serving a five-to-ten for assault with intent. But that was where it ended; they'd never picked him up; he had vanished into the blue.

"*¡Como no!*" said Mendoza softly. "*¿Cuanto apuestas*—how much do you bet?"

"Six years," said Palliser. "Where is he now?"

"Around. Obviously."

"He's got to have turned into a nut," said Trotwood excitedly, reminding them that he was there. He'd have simply loved to stay and watch them work it, but they showed him gently out, with fervent thanks. Carl Trotwood had broken the case for them, and they were grateful, but they would have to take it from there, the professionals.

"Six years," said Mendoza. The story said that Holland had been living with an aunt and uncle, Mr. and Mrs. William Holland, in Altadena. Palliser got out the phone book and looked; they were still listed.

"Delicate approach shot," said Mendoza, who had never played golf in his life. Lake got him the number and a rather shaky elderly voice answered. "Mr. Holland? Lieutenant Mendoza of the Los Angeles police. I'm sorry to remind you of that old murder case, sir, where your nephew was involved . . . Yes . . . Well, there may be some fresh evidence, and we'd like to talk to your nephew. Is he still living with you? . . . Oh, I see. Yes, please . . . Thank you very much, sir." He put the phone down. He said tersely to Palliser, "They weren't sure he'd recover fully, the doctors were afraid of irreparable brain damage, but he apparently got over it just fine. He dropped out of college and he's currently working on the maintenance crew at the Wilshire Country Club. Has an apartment in Hollywood."

"Let's go find him," said Palliser, equally terse.

The Wilshire Country Club was a sprawling piece of greenery surprisingly more or less in the middle of Hollywood, below Melrose, between June and Rossmore Streets. They took Palliser's car, in case they'd be bringing him back.

It was a nice spring day and there were a number of golfers out on the pretty green lawns. There was a clubhouse, empty, and a building for maintenance equipment. There, a big farmerish-looking man was working on one of the riding lawnmowers. Mendoza asked if Holland was working today.

The man straightened up and looked at them, and put down the wrench in his hand, substituted a pair of pliers. "Him," he said. "He got fired a month ago. Half the time never showed up, and acted queer as Dick's hatband when he did."

"What's the address?" asked Palliser back in the car.

"Leland Way."

That was the middle of old Hollywood, all much run down and showing its age. When they found it, it was one of the garish jerry-built little garden apartments, but minus a pool. Don Holland's apartment was at the back on the ground floor. Palliser shoved the bell, and they waited; nothing happened and he shoved it again. Mendoza reached past him and tried the door; it opened and they went in.

The little living room was in the wildest disorder, clothes, book and magazines scattered all over on every surface and the floor, and the room was crowded with furniture, a big stereo cabinet, a TV, oversized couch, two armchairs; but the first thing they saw was the knife. It was an ordinary big bread knife with a long serrated blade, and it hadn't been washed since the last time it had killed; it was covered with ugly dark-brown stains. It was lying on top of a dirty white shirt on the TV.

Don Holland was sitting in an armchair in front of the TV, but the TV wasn't on. He looked much, much older than the picture in *Master Detective*, which had been taken at his high school graduation; but he was only twenty-five now.

"Hello, Don," said Palliser quietly.

191

Holland looked up slowly. "Well, hello," he said, and a vaguely pleased smile came over his face.

"We'd like to talk to you," said Palliser. There was an unfolded newspaper on the floor, and he tore off the top page—which bore a large picture of Upchurch—and slid the knife onto it. "About this. We're police, Don."

"Oh," said Holland. Then he said rapidly, "The police tried, they were all good men, all good men, you know."

"Don," said Mendoza. "What did you want this knife for? What have you been using it for?"

"It's nice to have someone to talk to," said Holland, blinking. "When did you come? I don't remember. I haven't really had anyone to talk to for a long time. And it would help to talk, because I've been feeling—kind of confused."

"You go right ahead and talk, we'd like to listen, Don," said Palliser.

He smiled at them a little uncertainly. "You see, I never forgot Jeanie, of course. But for a while there, all that—was sort of at the back of my mind. But it's since her birthday—her birthday was March the seventh, and I took some flowers to her grave in Forest Lawn—yellow roses because they were her favorite—I couldn't stop thinking about him. He never paid for what he did to Jeanie."

"Seacarn," said Mendoza very softly.

"That's his name. I knew he was down there somewhere—around where they found his car. He was still there. And I had to kill him, for what he did to Jeanie. I've been out—nearly every day—hunting for him. Because I knew he had to be there. Somewhere down there. And I knew what he looked like, I'd recognize him."

"And did you?" asked Palliser conversationally.

Slowly he nodded. "Yes, I did. I found him—and I knew him right away—but you see, he's very clever. He can change his face so he looks different. At first, I knew it was him, and then he changed—he got away again—but I kept looking. And I found him again. I had to find him—to keep on finding him—to make him pay for Jeanie. But it's been—awfully confusing, you know. I'm glad to have someone to explain it to."

"We know some people you'll like talking to even better than us," said Palliser. "They understand confusing things like that, and maybe they'll help you understand it better. If you don't mind going somewhere to meet them."

"Oh, I don't mind at all, I don't seem to have really talked to anybody in a long while," said Holland dreamily.

The phone was in the kitchen. Mendoza went to use it, and fifteen minutes later the ambulance arrived. They followed it out to Cedars–Sinai. The psychiatrist they talked to, a bouncy little man named Steiner, was interested. "There could have been brain damage not immediately detectable," he said. "Just showing up. We'll have a look and find out. But it's an interesting case, Lieutenant. We'll look after him. I don't suppose it's likely to come to trial."

"That depends on you, Doctor," said Mendoza dryly.

"Yes, well," said Dr. Steiner, "I'm scarcely likely to tell a judge he's responsible for his actions."

Holland would probably end up in Atascadero. On the way back downtown Palliser said, "God. What a senseless damned random thing, those harmless fellows killed because he'd gone that far off the beam. And originally, take it back to beginnings, because they never caught up to Seacarn."

"The kind of thing that happens," said Mendoza. "The human nature we're here to deal with, John."

When he turned up Hamlin Place and at the top of it came to the impressive wrought-iron gates, he pushed the gadget on the dashboard and the gates swung open silently and majestically. But as he accelerated, the gates began to close again, and only a frantic reversal saved the Ferrari's nose from being smashed; they were heavy gates. Mendoza swore and tried the thing again; the gates opened and immediately closed. Something wrong with the damned electric eye, he thought. The only drawback to the marvelous mechanisms was that the more complex they were, the more could go wrong with them. The gates were, of course, operable manually, and he got out and opened them, drove through, got out and closed them again, and drove on up to the house.

Mairí's car wasn't in the garage, and he wondered where she was. He walked into the kitchen and found it empty; the whole house was silent. No twins came running. He left his hat on the kitchen table and went down the hall. He found Mairí just starting up the front stairs; she gave him a frosty glance. Wondering what he'd done, Mendoza went on into the living room. Here he found Alison lying back in his armchair with her feet up and her eyes closed, with two cats on her lap and two beside her and Cedric sound asleep on the floor beside the ottoman.

"*Querida*, there's something wrong with that damned electric eye, and—"

Alison opened one eye and squinted up at him. "Oh, are you telling me!" she said bitterly. "When I went out this morning, the damned gate let me get halfway through and then banged in the whole rear end of the Facel-Vega. It's running, but the garage says there's about three hundred dollars' worth of dents to be ironed out."

"*¡Por Dios!*" said Mendoza. "I never looked at your car—"

"And I didn't know Mairí was going out, or I'd have called to warn her. And when she went out, the gates let her out all right, but when she came back they smashed in the front of the Chevy and ruined her radiator, and the car had to be towed in to the garage. And she's so annoyed about it she's been talking broader and broader Scots ever since."

"*¡Caray!*" said Mendoza, amused.

"So I called the company, and the man said it probably just needs adjusting, and he'll come out tomorrow."

"Good."

"But our precious offspring, having attention called to the gates, wandered down there when nobody was looking and played around opening and shutting them, and of course when they got bored and came back to the house they left the gates open. And all the sheep got out."

"*¡Desastre!*" said Mendoza.

"Ken was up on the roof of their garage putting on shingles, and just happened to glance down the hill. He had an awful time rounding them up and getting them back in, they were starting down into Burbank— Well, it's not *that* funny, Luis! What a day! And the twins are confined to quarters. And if you'd like to take me out to dinner, I won't say no."

Glasser was off on Friday. They'd be glad to have Nick Galeano back, with business picking up a little. Overnight there had been a felony hit-run on Hill, a woman and child killed and another woman injured; she might be able to give them a description of the car, when she could be seen in the hospital.

There was still paperwork to be done on the Patterson case, and the other heisters to look for, and the new one that had gotten started yesterday. But Hackett came into Mendoza's office, sat down and lit a cigarette and said, "What you were telling me about that lawyer—you know, Luis, I still don't think we know the whole story on Parmenter. I've just got a funny feeling on that one."

"Oh, I've had the same thought," said Mendoza. He leaned back and blew smoke at the ceiling.

"Hunch?"

"No hunch." And detectives weren't supposed to work by hunches, but one reason that Luis Rodolfo Vicente Mendoza sometimes saw through a difficult case where logic failed was that he was prone to the hunches now and then. "Just a funny feeling, as you say."

"When you come to think of it, can you really see any of that—that furtive little bunch killing him? I know it wasn't intentional, he had a heart attack, but—even beating him up—"

"No, not men of action. But he didn't seem to know anybody else." The phone rang and Mendoza picked it up.

"It's the D.A.'s office," said Lake. "They want a conference about Upchurch."

"*¡Por Dios!* What's it got to do with me? It's their baby now." He had won the bet; Rosalie was spread all over front pages, and possibly would end up getting screen tests offered. "Oh, all right, all right. What time?"

"Three o'clock."

"Well, I suppose I'd better go and earn my pay for once." Hackett got up. "George hasn't been able to find out a single thing about that Fuller. At least our Dapper Dan missed last Sunday, I wonder if he's got a victim picked out for next Sunday."

"Don't borrow trouble, *chico*."

"And how in hell we'd ever catch up to that one . . ."

Grace and Palliser were now getting statements from the wives of the men involved with Goodis; the D.A. hadn't decided yet whether to charge them as accessories.

Mendoza was sitting there thinking about Parmenter, about any possible way to set up a trap for Dapper Dan— but his imagination failed him there—when Lake brought in a big handsome young fellow in uniform and a tall thin miserable-looking kid. "And what is this in aid of?" asked Mendoza.

The uniformed man almost shied back. He said humbly, apologetically, "I'm very sorry to disturb you, Lieutenant, but I figured it was the right place to come. I mean, we're supposed to do everything by the book, sir, and that's what I thought was right to do. To bring him here."

"How long have you been riding a squad—what's your name?"

"McConnell, sir. Dave McConnell. Thirty-two days, sir."

Mendoza grinned at him. "Well, not that I want to encourage insubordination, but just bear it in mind when you're talking to any brass that all of us started out riding a squad and there was a time when all of us had been wearing the uniform just thirty-two days. *¡Dios!* When I was riding a squad, this was a hell of a lot easier town to police than it is now. I don't envy you. So tell me why you've come to see me."

McConnell relaxed a little. "This kid," he said. "I was

stopped for a light at Woodlawn and Santa Barbara, and he came up to the squad and said he wanted to confess to a murder. And he gave me a gun."

"*¿Qué es esto?* Let's have it."

McConnell stepped closer and laid a gun on the desk. Mendoza looked at it with interest. "That's fine, McConnell—thanks, we'll take it from here. And you did right—going by the book."

"Thank you, sir." McConnell very nearly saluted, and with encouragement might have backed out; Mendoza, never especially concerned with protocol, didn't realize what a reputation he had on this force.

He looked at the kid. Not quite a kid: at least six-two, but gangling and skinny, probably looking younger than he was, with a narrow weak face. "Suppose you sit down," he said. Silently the kid sat down in the chair beside the desk. "Like to tell me your name?"

"Tommy—Tommy Hernandez."

Mendoza got up and went out to see who was in. Wanda was typing a report; he lifted a finger and she followed him back to his office. "Tommy Hernandez. He says he wants to talk about a murder. What about it, Tommy?"

He looked ready to cry. He wasn't a bad-looking boy, in a girlish way; he had black hair a little untidy but not overlong, neat features. He said in a thin voice, "I been thinking about it ever since, I just can't stop thinking about it, and I never felt so bad in my life. Mr. Robillard—he was just the nicest guy in the world, I'd never do anything to hurt Mr. Robillard. He used to help me with lots of things when he hadn't no call to. It was the money, that was all. I just wanted the money."

"All right," said Mendoza. "Tell it from the beginning."

He sat there with his head down, and he said miserably, "I couldn't get a job, I mean to keep. I got the diploma when I graduated, and I thought that meant I knew something, I didn't do too bad all through school. But I got the job at the gas station, and after a couple days the boss said damn stupid kid, they don't teach you enough arithmetic to make change, and he fired me. I couldn't learn to work that register thing at all. And Mom said try the employment agency so I did, and they gave me a kind of test and I got all mixed up, I couldn't make out the questions, and the guy said I was func— func something illiterate and it'd be hard to find me a job. And then I got a job at the market, putting things in bags and carrying them out for people, only I couldn't do that right either, they got mad at me because I mixed things up, you're supposed like to put certain things in the same bags and I couldn't read what it said on the packages, all different kinds of letters. And I wanted to help Mom—she always needs money so bad. See, my dad died a couple of years ago. He got sick and died. And Mom has to work, she works at a place where they make ladies' dresses. And I got three brothers, they're all younger'n me, Billy's only ten, and they need things." He looked up at Mendoza, and there was a terrible bewilderment in his dark eyes. "Last year," he said, and paused, "last year, before I graduated, everybody thought I was great. I did pretty good on the basketball team. Everybody cheered when I made a basket. And then all of a sudden I'm no good for anything. And I wanted to get some money for Mom, and I thought if I wasn't smart enough to keep a job, maybe I could be a crook and just steal some. If I wasn't no good anyway—

"And I remembered how Mis' Flowers always brings out the cafeteria money in the afternoon. I guess I just didn't think about anybody else maybe bein' there. I knew which was her car."

"Where did you get the gun?" asked Mendoza.

"Oh, it was my dad's, to scare burglars with. I think Mom forgot it was there, on the closet shelf. I was just going to scare Mis' Flowers with it, to get the money. I didn't know there were any bullets in it." He gave a sudden dry sob. "I never meant to shoot it! But when I heard Mr. Robillard yell—I never knew he was there—it scared me and I turned around and it went off all by itself—I never knew a gun could go off all by itself like that—"

Mendoza sighed. An automatic could be a tricky sort of gun, and a lot of them had a very light pull. If there was a charge left up the spout ready to go . . .

He began to cry. "It's gonna hurt my mom awful bad—find out I did a thing like that—I never meant to do a thing like that—and Mr. Robillard . . ."

Wanda sighed too. And this was another senseless random thing, and what would happen to Tommy now was in the lap of the gods.

But later on, when the warrant had been applied for and he'd been booked into jail and Wanda was typing a report on it, Mendoza said to her, "Don't mention rehabilitation services in prison."

"Don't they ever work?"

"It's a nice idea in theory. About once in a thousand times. What annoys the hell out of me is these damned schools that don't even teach the kids to read, and then hand them the nice diploma that says they're educated. Maybe they'll teach him to read in prison." He wandered back to his office sadly. Cases like that depressed him.

Higgins was feeling annoyed and frustrated. The hotel-in-quotes on Temple was a sleazy sort of place, and tenants came and went without any sort of record being kept. All the manager, the desk clerk, whatever he called himself, could say was how long Fuller had been there, that he didn't seem to have a regular job but paid for his room on time. There hadn't been anything in the room to suggest any kind of background for Fuller; in fact it was just a little mystery, who he'd been and why anybody had shot him and who that had been.

He and Landers had been here again this afternoon, talking to the various tenants who were on Social Security, who had night jobs, and they hadn't gotten any new information. They were just thinking of knocking off and going back to the office when Higgins remembered that he hadn't talked to the man in the next room to Fuller's. Gillespie. He went over to the desk, where the manager–desk clerk was sitting reading a paperback Western, and asked him if Mr. Gillespie had come back yet. Another mystery, that one taking off for a few days now and then; maybe off on a drunk.

"Yeah," said the manager. "He came back last night, I was just goin' in my place," and he nodded to the door behind the counter, evidently his private domain, "when he come in. I nearly stepped out again, tell him about Fuller, and then I figured what the hell. But he ain't been out today."

Climbing the creaky old bare stairs, Higgins thought they might as well shove this in Pending now and stop wasting time on it; they were never going to get anywhere. He went down the hall and rapped on Gillespie's door. Almost at once it opened. Gillespie was a short spare man with a bald head. "Mr. Gillespie?"

"Yes?" he said in a quiet voice.

Higgins reached for his badge. "I'd like to ask you a few questions—"

Gillespie slammed the door in his face, and ten seconds later there was a loud crack from behind it. "My God!" said Higgins, stupefied.

Landers came pounding up the stairs. "Was that a shot? What—"

"Nearly gave me a heart attack. What the hell?" They tried the door and it opened. Across the bed lay the short spare body of Mr. Gillespie; he had shot himself in the head, and he was dead. The gun had fallen out of his hand; it was an old Hi-Standard .22.

The manager came running. "Was that a shot? Oh, my God!"

"Ten years off my life," said Higgins. But of course, maybe it solved their little mystery. When Marx and Horder got there, to take the routine pictures, he asked, "Did the morgue send over the slug from the other one here on Tuesday? Have you looked at it? Well, was it a twenty-two?"

"George," said Marx, "you saw the corpse. Does a twenty-two blow off half a man's head? It was a three fifty-seven magnum."

"That just makes all of this more confusing," said Higgins. They went back to the office and told Mendoza that the little mystery had escalated, and what had happened.

"Just run through that once more . . . Well, I can only think you both need a vacation, George. The manager told you that Gillespie hadn't heard about Fuller yet, didn't know there were police around, about that. You march up to him and show him a badge, say you want to ask questions. *Obvio*, he thought you were after him. He's probably wanted somewhere. Ask NCIC."

"Damn it, that never— Of course."

"You don't realize," said Mendoza, "what an intimidating fellow you are, is all."

Higgins got home that Friday night just as the light was fading; next month they'd be on daylight saving and he'd be home before dark. The little Scotty Brucie came to meet him as he shut the garage door, and he went into the kitchen to find Mary at the stove. He kissed her and she said, "Reasonably good day?"

"A funny day," said Higgins. "Some pretty peculiar things are happening on the job lately, if you ask me. I think I'll have a drink before dinner. I had a little shock this afternoon." And hearing his voice, Steve Dwyer came out of his room; he had shot up another inch in the last couple of months, and looked more like Bert than ever.

"Hey, George, look at the great shots I got of that sunset over the mountains, that new filter is really something."

Margaret Emily was playing on the living-room floor with a big stuffed dog, and Laura was practicing the piano, loud. But her teacher said she was some kind of musical genius so they had to put up with it.

Higgins went to build himself a drink before he admired Steve's pictures.

"Well, it might be fun," said Roberta. "I got all this litera-ture from the local obedience club today. She's really pretty good." They looked at the big black German shepherd Trina on the floor between them. Roberta had just come back from tucking the baby into bed. "I never saw the sense of regular dog shows, but the obedience thing, to show how intelligent they are, that's interesting. The show's in June, in Pasadena. I can work with her a lot more in the meantime. And the entrance fee's only ten dollars for the novice class."

"Go ahead." Palliser smiled at her.

"Would you like that, girl? Like to go to the show and have everybody see how smart you are?" Trina thumped her tail enthusiastically.

"If she does take first prize it'll be all your doing, you're the one who's trained her."

"The only thing is, it's on a Sunday and you couldn't come. How much seniority do you have to have to get Sundays off?"

"It goes by rote, you know that. Just be thankful I'm not on night watch. Rich Conway is damned annoyed about that, but maybe it'll settle him down some."

She laughed. "Well, the bride and groom will be back soon. She seemed very nice, I do hope they'll be happy."

"We'll be damned glad to have Nick back," said Palliser feelingly.

The woman at the hospital, the only one who'd survived the hit-run, was Mrs. Margarita Patillo. She had a broken leg and a sprained wrist, and she'd been knocked out with a con-cussion, but now she could be talked to. They had her propped up a little, with the leg in traction, and she looked quite alert and sensible, if her face was drawn with grief. She was a woman in her forties, still attractive. There was a man about the same age sitting beside the bed when Conway came in.

"Oh, I'll go out," he said when Conway introduced himself.

"Not on my account, sir, I just want to ask Mrs. Patillo what she can tell us about the accident."

"Accident!" she said. "This is my husband, I guess he can stay. Only don't try to tell the man I'm crazy, Joe."

"You've got an imagination, Rita." He grinned at her faintly.

"I know what I know," she said obstinately, and turned to Conway. The tears welled up in her dark eyes; she said, "I suppose you know that I was with my niece—Mrs. Ina Rush—and her daughter Pam. Oh, Pam! She was only eight—"

"Yes, we know that, Mrs. Patillo. Did you get a look at the car at all?"

"That isn't going to do you any good," she told him. "You listen to me. Ina found out about that bum a year after she married him—he was always chasing other women and gambling—but she tried to make the marriage work on account of Pam. But it just got too bad, and she divorced him six months ago. And the judge gave her four hundred a month alimony and child support, and Jim Rush was mad as—as fire about it. He makes pretty good money, he drives a refuse truck for the city. But he's got another woman on the string and there's nothing he'd like better than to be rid of Ina and Pam."

"You know," said Conway, "unless you've got some evidence, that's slander."

"Just what I been telling her," said Patillo.

"Men," she said. "You listen. I know it was late for Pam, but I don't get off work till three, and there was this movie we all wanted to see. Joe said he'd get his own dinner. We went to the show, and we got out about six forty-five and we went up to that restaurant on Hill for dinner. And it was when we came out—Ina was parked in the lot across the street —not much traffic, it was about eight-thirty—it happened. The street was empty—nothing any direction—and we started across, and all of a sudden I heard an engine start up with a big zoom, and that car pulled out from the curb down the block—from the curb, mind you—and headed straight for us!"

"You're telling me it was deliberate. How sure are you?"

"I'm sure," she said grimly.

"You're not going to tell me you recognized the driver," said Conway.

"No, I'm not such a fool," she said candidly. "It was too dark. I heard Ina scream, and I tried to reach for Pam, but it was all too quick—" She gave a shuddering sigh.

"I take it Mrs. Rush wasn't in contact with her ex-husband. How would he have known where she'd be, to try to run her down?"

"Now that's the big question," she said. "I don't know, but he did. He knows girl friends of hers, he's a smooth talker, he could even have hired a private detective if he figured he could get rid of her—"

"Oh, Rita," said her husband. "It's just a damned awful thing about Ina and Pam, but you've got an imagination—"

"I know!"

"The car?" asked Conway.

"Oh, it wasn't his car," she said scornfully, "he wouldn't use that, in case he didn't kill her and she could say it was him. It was a big station wagon, I don't know what kind, it was either gray or tan . . ."

Conway sighed and continued to make notes. He'd just had it on the grapevine tonight that his best girl, who was a policewoman stationed at Hollenbeck precinct, had started dating a detective in the Vice office. He was feeling annoyed about it, but there wasn't a damned thing he could do about it.

At ten-forty that night, Mr. and Mrs. Paul Warren and their eight-year-old daughter Mary Ann came out of the Baker Marionette Theater on First Street. Mary Ann wasn't usually up that late, but it wasn't a school night and she was crazy about marionettes. It was a prebirthday treat, because she was only having a small party next Tuesday, when she'd be nine.

Paul Warren had an excellent legal practice in Glendale, but he was also an ex-fullback for UCLA and kept himself in shape without being a fanatic about it; he was six two and a solid hundred and ninety.

They were late coming out, because Molly Warren had dropped the case for her glasses under the seat in the theater, and a couple of ushers took a while to find it. There hadn't been a very big audience; not everybody went for marionettes, and Paul Warren had been rather bored, but he liked to please his womenfolk.

They went across a largely empty parking lot to his car, a year-old Monte Carlo, and Mary Ann climbed into the back seat as Warren unlocked the doors.

And then a voice said behind him, "Excuse me."

A man had come up from the side alley, a tallish shadowy figure, hat pulled down to shade his face. He had a large Doberman pinscher with him on a leash. "Yes?" said Warren, surprised.

"Excuse me, but this is a trained attack dog and I'll set him on you if you don't give me your money. Come on, hurry up!"

Warren froze. He heard Molly utter a little gasp. He looked at the dog; he knew Dobes. He started to reach for his wallet. And then Mary Ann, hearing the voices, opened the door and jumped out of the car. And the dog gave a great whine of rapture and yanked the leash loose and ran up to her, licking her face and waggling his tailless rear end like mad, and Mary Ann threw her arms around him and cried, "Oh, Daddy, he's just like Rusty!"

Warren hesitated no longer. He brought one up from the ground, and landed square on the jaw, and the man fell over backward onto the blacktop and lay very still.

"What?" said Mendoza. "I didn't get that." There were phones all over Alison's big house, and he'd just been undressing, was standing in the master suite with just shorts on. Alison was splashing noisily in the bathroom.

"I said we didn't know what the hell to do about the dog," said Conway. "Animal Control is shut down for the night. It's at the jail, one of the jailers said he'd take it out for a walk now and then. It's a nice friendly big dog. The guy's name is Charles Gage, he came to but he acted kind of dazed, and the doctor at the jail said he might have concussion. I suppose you can turn the dog over to Animal Control tomorrow, but damn it, they don't keep them long, do they? It's a nice dog. If this Gage has any family to claim it . . . But it was the funniest damned thing, Lieutenant, after all we'd heard about this savage beast—such a nice little girl, nice family, and the dog was all over her, wagging its rear end and licking her face. The woman said they'd just lost an old Doberman sixteen years old, and the little girl had been heartbroken."

"Yes, I see," said Mendoza.

Conway was laughing again. "The savage beast. Well, it was funny."

"Very," said Mendoza. "We'll sort it out tomorrow."

TEN

Charles Gage looked at Mendoza and said, "So we come to the end of the road. God, it's like a Greek play." They had transferred him to the jail infirmary for observation, and the doctor had said there was a mild concussion but he would be all right. He was in a tiny narrow slot of a room, only big enough for the hospital bed and a chair. He was a nearly handsome man in his early forties, tall, with dark hair, regular features, but a very ordinary man, a man you wouldn't look at twice. He was wearing the tan cotton jail uniform, and he looked white and ill, whatever the jail doctor said.

He gave Mendoza a very faint smile and said, "I knew it was all up when the little girl got out of the car. I think Bruno misses Caroline as much as I do."

"Caroline."

"My daughter. She died of leukemia last year. She was nine."

"Well, Mr. Gage," said Mendoza, "you had a novel idea for pulling heist jobs. We didn't have any way to trace you at all."

"It was a crazy idea," said Gage sadly. "But I've been about crazy. What with everything."

"Suppose you tell me about it."

"I don't know why the police would want to listen to the story of my life," said Gage listlessly. He was lying on the made bed fully dressed; they would be transferring him back to a jail cell after Mendoza had talked to him. "I don't want to sound sorry for myself, but— God, everything seemed to happen at once—as if God Himself had turned His back on me. And up to then, everything had been pretty good, a good life. Well, I won't say that Helen and I didn't have differences, but we got along. She was always a little jealous of Caroline, but she was a good mother, and we had a nice house—West Hollywood—and the business was doing fine— and the nice big back yard for Bruno—I had it made, at forty-one."

"What business?" asked Mendoza.

"I've got an import and giftware shop at the Farmer's Market in Hollywood. Not cheap stuff, all good quality—you have to know how to buy, but experience tells you what's going to sell. I had a girl working for me, and I thought she was a nice girl—very efficient girl, named Doris King. Everything—going—fine." He sat up a little straighter. Mendoza had lit a cigarette and he said apologetically, "Could I bum one of those from you? Thanks. I haven't been buying any lately—too damned expensive." He smoked in silence for a while, and said, "Of course, the very worst was Caroline. I suppose I had spoiled her—the one ewe lamb. She lived seven months, and the medical bills piled up— God, God, way over a hundred thousand bucks—if they could have done something, that wouldn't have mattered, but of course they couldn't. She died just a little over a year ago. And then Helen changed, got restless, she began to pick fights with me over nothing—she always did say I was a stodgy slowpoke, never wanted to go out anywhere—well, I never have been one for that, I guess it was pretty slow and dull for her, when Caroline— Well, she just changed. And she decided she wanted a divorce. She said she wanted some kind of better life while she was still young enough to enjoy it." He was sitting on the edge of the bed now, head down, cigarette dangling loose between his fingers; he took a last drag and put it out carefully in the dime-store ashtray, and Mendoza offered him another. "Thanks. Well, she had a smart lawyer, and I guess he had an exaggerated idea about the business, a judge gave her five hundred a month alimony. And the next thing was that that King girl cleaned out the store bank account. You'll think I was a fool, but she'd been with me for five years, I trusted her. I'd given her the power to sign checks on it because sometimes wholesale orders would get delivered when I wasn't there, or I'd be away on a buying trip when the utility bills came due. You see? I never dreamed she could do such a thing—but she got in with some crook, fell hard for him—the police found out all about it—and they took me for over twelve thousand dollars, all the backlog, the net profits to go back into the business. The police never got them, they traced them to Hawaii and then they just disappeared.

"Helen didn't want the house, maybe she had some conscience and saw how I'd be left—there was still thirty-seven thousand owing on it and she knew I couldn't swing that, I was still paying off the medical bills, and what with the alimony I knew I couldn't keep the house—the payments— Not that I suppose she knew, the lease was up at the store, I had to sign a new one and they raised the ante, nine hundred a month for a twenty-by-forty space facing on Fairfax. I knew I had to sell the house. It was then I did it the first time," said Gage suddenly.

"How did it happen to occur to you?" asked Mendoza curiously.

"Helen had moved out. She'd gotten an apartment in Santa Monica and a job—she was a legal secretary before we were married, and she got a good job down there. I'd just had an offer for the house—we had to drop the price—and I was so damned worried about money," said Gage. "So—

damn—worried. The five hundred a month had to come right off the top. Well, I'd taken Bruno out for a walk that night as usual, and I saw these people going up to a car just ahead of me, and the woman looked at Bruno and sort of shied a little. My good God, I don't know where the damn fool idea came from, but so many people are afraid of Dobermans—and for God's sake, the man handed over the money like a lamb. I felt like a damned fool when he did— good God, I was in a bad enough fix as it was, I didn't have to turn into a crook! Well"—he took a long drag on the cigarette—"I sold the house, and I applied all the money to the medical bills, which cut it down to only about thirty-five thousand I still owed. Only!" He looked at Mendoza. "I don't know why you're listening to all this."

"Go on, Mr. Gage."

"I had a hell of a time to find a place to rent where I could keep Bruno. I finally found a duplex, it's on Kensington up toward Elysian Park, an old run-down neighborhood, but the owner lives on the other side and he said he'd be glad of a dog there to scare burglars. But it's just a little yard. I took him for a walk every night. I was so *damned* strapped for money," said Gage, bitterly. "The rent at the store, and the utility bills had doubled since last year, and business was way off with inflation so high and wholesale prices up—even the tourist season didn't help—and that goddamned girl left me with no backlog, I couldn't order new stock—and the alimony every month—the rent at the duplex is three hundred—"

"Many a man," said Mendoza, blowing smoke at the ceiling, "has been driven to crime through desperation."

"You could damn well say I was," said Gage. "But of course I must have been crazy. Just crazy. You see, I thought afterward—about that first time, I thought it could be that those people needed that money just as badly as I did. But when it got—really a little desperate—the business way off, the stock getting low, and I couldn't hire another employee, and I was doing without lunch—oh, there were a lot of times when eating money was hard to come by—I thought, people who could afford to go to expensive theaters anywhere, the money I'd take wouldn't be food and rent money, at least."

"So that was why. I see."

"That was why." Gage lay back on the bed, and turned his face away. "One haul I got—it was about forty dollars—went to pay for Bruno's rabies and booster shots. That may sound crazy to you, but—you have a dog—you have responsibilities. Bruno was all I had left. I didn't have enough money for a decent meal that week. Soup and cereal—and even milk—the utilities are extra at the duplex—" And he said draggingly, drearily, "But the very worst—I know you'll send me to prison for it, and I deserve that—but the very worst is what I've done to Bruno. The dog didn't know—doing anything wrong. And now—there's no one to take care of him. People we knew—mostly Helen's friends—like her, don't care for dogs, know anything about—" Gage was silent. "I've killed him, you know. My Bruno. He's only five. There's no one to look after him. Just because I was such a goddamned fool, I've killed him, and I deserve to be hanged for that."

"You know," said Mendoza consideringly, "I think there may be a solution, Mr. Gage. It is queer how things happen. You just happening to walk up to the Warrens last night. It just goes to show"—he grinned at Gage—"which the atheists so stubbornly deny, that there is something arranging life in patterns after all."

And of course it was well known to everyone who knew him that Mendoza was a cat man; and they were busy enough at Robbery-Homicide, with two new heists last night. But he drove up to Glendale and found the Warrens' house, which was a pleasant big house on a quiet street with a large fenced back yard, and he told the Warrens about Charles Gage.

"The poor devil down on his luck all right," said Warren. "I can see where he got to feeling desperate. I wonder if he'd like me to represent him in court."

"He'll be given an attorney."

"Yes, I know, but those boys are either just out of law school and still wet behind the ears, or drones just marking time," said Warren. "There'll be his business to close out, that lease to deal with—and my God, there'll be some way to get that alimony reduced, that's outrageous when the woman's got a good job, and there aren't any children. What do you think he might get?"

Mendoza was smoking lazily. "It's a first charge, but a felony. He might draw a one-to-three, and be out on parole in nine months or so. He's not worried about that, Mr. Warren. He's worried sick about the dog, because there's no one to take care of the dog. The dog's in the Ann Street shelter. He told me he deserved to be hanged for that."

Warren looked at his wife, and they exchanged a little smile. "We'll look after the dog," said Warren. "I'd better call the shelter right away, they don't keep them long there. He looked like a nice Dobe, and"—he laughed—"he certainly did take to Mary Ann, didn't he?"

"Thank you very much, Mr. Warren," said Mendoza. "That's just what I hoped you'd say."

"Well, I don't see that there could be much in this Rush thing," said Hackett doubtfully. "It'd be a chancy way to try to kill somebody, fake a hit-run. We can take a look at Rush, see what he looks like, but probably the Patillo woman is just using her imagination."

"*Conforme.* But we'd better look, just in case."

Business continued to hum along. Atlanta was going to extradite Rogers, and somebody would be out, probably next week, to pick him up. On the two new heists, at a drugstore and a small independent market, they had fair descriptions. The inquest on the mysterious Fuller was set for Monday. Higgins had sent the equally mysterious Mr. Gillespie's prints to NCIC; they hadn't had a kickback on that yet. Powell was being arraigned on Monday; the D.A. was calling it murder two, but Mendoza said cynically that that was just for show, there'd be a plea bargain and it would get reduced to voluntary manslaughter. He wondered if Rosalie would get a film contract out of it.

The paperwork on the Patterson case was about cleared up. That crew would probably come up for arraignment on Tuesday or Wednesday. What legal disposition would be made of Holland was up to the D.A. and the doctors, but the psychiatric evaluation would undoubtedly put him in Atascadero after a court hearing.

About four o'clock that Saturday afternoon Higgins had just brought in a heist suspect to question, when the kickback from NCIC came in. NCIC didn't know anything about Robert Gillespie; his prints weren't on file with them. "That's funny," said Higgins. "I tell you, Luis, I never had such a shock in my life. Why the hell *did* he kill himself?"

"You'd better have a close look at his personal effects again. We don't know what he was up to when he took off now and then," said Mendoza. "He could have been mixed up with dope running—or prostitution—"

"And living in that fleabag hotel?"

"Maybe he was an international spy. But they usually have cyanide capsules ready, don't they?"

"Very funny," said Higgins.

When Mendoza got home that night, the electric eye was adjusted and working smoothly just as it should. But Alison informed him that Ken had discovered that the nearest professional sheep shearer lived somewhere above Santa Barbara and would charge a hundred dollars and expenses to come all the way down here to shear five sheep. "He said he'll get a book from the library and learn how to do it so next year—"

"My good God," said Mendoza, "what you do get us into —talk about one thing leading to another!"

On Sunday morning Higgins thought it was worth an hour's time to take Mendoza's advice. He was curious about Mr. Gillespie. He had put a police seal on the door of the room in case they wanted to take another look, and he got there about nine o'clock and first went through all the drawers in the chest. The room was only about nine by twelve, and held the bed, the chest, a nightstand and a small armchair. The bathroom was down the hall. There wasn't anything in the drawers but clean underwear, shirts, ties, socks, handkerchieves: fair middle-priced quality. There was one extra suit hanging in the closet, three pairs of slacks, with two pairs of shoes, black and brown, on the floor. There were about a dozen library books, between a cheap pair of bookends, on the chest, and some magazines in the drawer of the nightstand. And a funny mixture those were: *Car Life, Coinage, Fate, Country Life* and *American Astrology.* The library books were even queerer: historical fiction, psychic research, classic crimes and a book on the history of winemaking. There was no rhyme or reason to be gotten out of that. There were three suitcases in the closet, and they all looked empty, but he felt carefully at sides and bottoms, and in the third one discovered that the bottom lining was loose, fastened down with Scotch tape. He pulled the tape off, lifted the lining, and looked at a respectable amount of nice green cash.

"I'll be damned," he muttered, and took it out to count it. It was all in tens and twenties, and it amounted to a little over nine hundred dollars. He decided it wasn't enough for a ransom payment or part of a bank heist, and too much for an ordinary heist or a burglary. He put it aside, felt again in all the suitcase pockets, and was rewarded with a small stiff card tucked in one of the side pockets. He looked at it. It was old and shredded at the corners, and the date on it was June 1974. It was a library card, made out in Gillespie's name, for the library in Stamford, Connecticut.

And that was all there was.

He took the cash back to the office to stash away as evidence, and Mendoza was interested.

"I wonder if it'd be worthwhile to ask the Stamford force if they know him," said Higgins.

"Explore every avenue," said Mendoza. "There's a new one down, by the way—Art and Tom went out on it."

The new homicide was a very messy one. It was a house on Mott Street, an old frame place with no grass or bushes in front, and needing paint. The squad-car man was Gomez, and he looked sick when he told them what to expect. "The visiting nurse found them and called in."

The house had a combination living-dining room, two bedrooms with a bathroom between, a square kitchen. It was in a shambles. Every drawer had been pulled out and dumped, clothes yanked down from closet poles, pictures torn off the walls. In the middle of the wreckage were the two bodies and quite a lot of blood.

The bodies were those of two very aged black people, and the first thought in Hackett's and Landers' minds was that there hadn't been any necessity to kill them; they couldn't have put up any fight at all. The old man had been stabbed as he sat in a wheelchair; he couldn't have weighed ninety pounds. The old woman was even thinner and frailer; she lay face down against one wall, and had probably been stabbed too. They could conclude that right away, for the knife had been left— an ordinary kitchen knife, bloody, in the middle of the living-room floor.

"Christ," said Landers.

They couldn't do anything until the lab had gotten at it. They called for a mobile unit, and went out and sat in the squad. The visiting nurse was shaken and pale, and nurses didn't react that way often. She was a competent-looking middle-aged woman with frosted blond hair, and she was voluble, if she couldn't tell them much that might be relevant to the murder.

"Mr. and Mrs. Eggers," she said. "William and Clara. Oh, my God, to see them like that—and the worst of it is, they weren't going to be here much longer. They weren't fit to be alone, and we'd arranged for them to go into a rest home."

She pressed a handkerchief to her mouth. "He was ninety-four and she was nearly ninety. They'd both been schoolteachers, he was a principal once, they were so proud of that, of getting an education, it wasn't so easy all those years ago—they were always telling how their parents just missed being born into slavery. But they'd been retired nearly thirty years, and back then teachers didn't get paid much, they just got along on Social Security, they didn't have anything—never had any children. He was nearly helpless, and she wasn't much better. They had the meals-on-wheels service, and I came three times a week to give them baths—"

"When were you here last?" asked Hackett.

"Thursday. Thursday afternoon. And when I came today— the front door all broken in—to think of them ending like that, when they'd been good honest hardworking people all their lives—I've gotten more and more nervous of coming into neighborhoods like this, I expect when they bought the house it was a decent street, but— They bought the house in nineteen-twenty, that's before I was born . . ."

Hackett, looking at the street, reflected that L.A. had changed in that piece of time: sixty-odd years, God, what had the street looked like then? A pleasant little house among others similar, on a narrow quiet street in downtown L.A., long before the city had amassed a million population. Now, the ancient houses were ready to fall down, the street was neglected and full of potholes, and a mongrel dog with its ribs showing was nosing along the gutter. There wasn't anybody out to stare at the police vehicles, exhibit curiosity; the people down here didn't like cops, or were afraid of them.

"It's just too pitiful," she said.

But of course it was the kind of street where the kind of people lived who might do a thing like this.

"My God," said Landers, "but anybody should have known they wouldn't have any money, anything valuable. You'd think."

"Things relative," said Hackett. "Maybe they had a little more than some along here, Tom."

It had been a very crude, hasty job; the lab might give them something right away.

The morgue wagon drew up to the curb silently, behind the lab truck.

At a little past two o'clock on Sunday, a squad called in an attempted rape, and Mendoza and Higgins went out on it in a hurry. It was an apartment house up on Glendale Avenue, an old red-brick place looking solid and comfortable, and the apartment was at the front downstairs.

"I thought I'd better call even if I wasn't hurt," said Eleanor Golinsky cheerfully, "because that guy is obviously a nut and ought to be tucked away before he hurts somebody. And I never had such a surprise in my life—me, not exactly the green girl from the country, and I like to think I've got some judgment of people!" She grinned at them, but she was still a little shaken. She was a big girl, at least five eight and sturdily built, with brown hair in a short no-nonsense cut, a plain round face, bright brown eyes behind tortoiseshell glasses. "Whoosh!" she said, appraising them, dismissing Mendoza as a fop, admiring Higgins' muscles. "I'll never trust my own judgment again. But he was plausible—God, he was so plausible and polite, anybody would have believed him! But he didn't know I know some judo."

"You're very lucky to have gotten away from him, Miss Golinsky," said Higgins. There wasn't any immediate point in telling her that he'd already hurt quite a few girls. "We can guess what he told you, but let's hear it from the beginning."

"Sure," she said. "I was getting ready to go to work—sheesh, I'm nearly an hour late and I never called Mr. Boggs, he'll have gone up in a sheet of flame—I'm a checker at a Safeway on Silver Lake—going to night school to make up enough credits to get my phys-ed teacher's certificate. Keeps me busy. Anyway, I was just dressed when he rang the bell—and talk about gentlemanly! Nobody would have suspected him of anything, and as for being afraid of him, hah, it is to laugh. Nice-looking fella, tall, dark, and dressed up to the nines." She flicked a glance at Mendoza's dapper tailoring, as if in comparison. "He said . . ." It was the same tale, of course, the misplaced sister, the letter brought out as if to check the address, the apologetic bewilderment, the request to call a taxi. "Never so surprised in my life," she said, "when he pulled that knife and reached for me. Well, I'm not going to tell you I wasn't scared, I saw what he had in mind, and I was scared to death, but I tried to keep my head—and like I say I know some judo. I also remembered what Mother always said and the first thing I did was to aim a good hard kick at him—bad luck I landed too low, but I don't think he liked it. You can see I'm pretty big and strong, and I got him in a judo hold once but he had enough height on me to get away—he dropped the knife and I kicked it under the couch and grabbed up a vase from the end table, nearest thing to hand, and cracked him over the head—darn it, I liked that vase too, but what the heck if it saved my virtue—and the first time I'd gotten hold of him I'd torn his jacket, and I think by then he just wanted to get away—"

"With some reason," said Mendoza, amused.

"He got the door open and ran, and you know, I darn near started after him—I was good and mad by then—and then reason, as they say, prevailed, and I locked the door and called for cops."

"Well, we're very glad you weren't hurt, Miss Golinsky." Higgins was moving the couch out to retrieve the knife; he slid it into an evidence bag. "He's a dangerous man. We've been chasing him for some time without any luck. All we've got is his description and the M.O.—"

"Come again."

"His *modus operandi*. The gimmick about the sister."

"Oh," she said. "Well, if it'll do you any good, in the general melee he dropped his prop. I suppose when I tore his jacket—I think he'd put it back in that pocket just before I let him in. I found it on the floor just before the Marines arrived," and she smiled at the squad-car man.

"What? His—"

"That letter he was waving around, supposed to be from his sister." She picked it up from the coffee table and handed it to Higgins.

It was a handwritten envelope addressed to Mrs. Cheryl Stack, at an address on Hillside Avenue in Hollywood.

The house was an old bungalow on that old street, on a corner, and reasonably well kept up, with lawn in front. "How exactly do we play this?" asked Higgins as Mendoza shoved the doorbell.

"By ear."

The woman who came to the door was middle-aged, plump, with a placid face. She looked at them enquiringly. "Mrs. Stack?" asked Mendoza.

"That's right."

He showed her the badge. "Police officers. I wonder if you can tell me how—"

He had the letter in his hand ready to show her, but at sight of the badge the small puzzlement left her eyes and she said, "Oh, it's about that arson case, I suppose. Well, I should think you'd know better than to try to get hold of Douglas on a work day. But there, excuse me, I expect policemen work regular hours and you wouldn't realize—he's at work, at the fire station, of course. But there again"—she considered—"could be you didn't know where he got transferred."

"Douglas Stack?" said Higgins tentatively.

"Well, who else are we talking about? My son Douglas, that's who you want to see, isn't it? He used to be at the station on Third, but last month he got transferred to the one on Jefferson downtown. I don't know why he was always set on being a fireman, the crazy hours they have to work."

"My God," said Higgins, "he was operating in Hollywood's territory and then they sent him downtown and he started prowling around there. Of all the—and a *fireman*—they have pretty stiff requirements, but—"

"But not," said Mendoza, "all the psychological testing we

run on prospective cops, George. One thing, if he's due on the job sometime soon, he'll still be carrying the marks of Miss Golinsky's battle for her virtue."

The captain of the fire station on Jefferson was incredulous. "Stack? My God, he's been on the department for four years, I had his record when he got transferred, of course, and there's not a mark against him. Very reliable man. A little moody, maybe, but one of the boys—I can't believe this."

"Well, we want to talk to him at least, there's a definite link," said Mendoza diplomatically. But they didn't have to do much talking: when Douglas Stack showed up to go on duty at four o'clock he was wearing his uniform, but he bore several deep angry gashes on one temple and was limping slightly. "And damn all the rules and regulations," said Mendoza softly as they saw him come in, "that suit will be in his car and we'll have to get a warrant before we can open a door."

But they took him in, and called Eleanor Golinsky down to take a look at him. "That's him all right," she said, "and I see I marked him. Good." Tomorrow they would bring in all the other girls, and they would recognize him too.

He was, as all the girls had said, an attractive man if not exactly handsome: young, tall, well set up, with presence enough and sufficient educational background to put up that good front. He could have attracted the girls easily enough. But a surprising number of the violent rapists were of the same ilk; that was quite irrelevant to what made them tick.

They couldn't get him to say anything for quite some time; and then he seemed to get impatient with all the repetitious questions and said, "It was Sally. I never did anything like that until that damn little bitch walked out on me."

"Sally who?" asked Mendoza.

"Sally Forcell. She was my girl ever since high school. I'd always been good enough before, till she ran into that dude with the foreign car and all the loot. Kicked me in the teeth and took off with him. I guess"—he looked at them from under his brows—"I started to feel all women were like that.

I had to get back at Sally."

It was the opening move in the gambit of trying to claim insanity, of course. It wasn't likely he'd get away with that, when such obvious plotting had gone into achieving the rapes. He would get the psychiatric evaluation, but nobody was going to think this one was crazy. They booked him into jail, and were both late home.

At nine o'clock Piggott called Mendoza to say that the warrant for his car had come through; it had been towed in, and they had looked. His natty suit and white shirt were there, only the suit wasn't so natty, with a pocket nearly torn off.

"And isn't that gratifying," said Mendoza. "I must remember to call Barth in the morning. His mistake, of course, was in picking on Miss Golinsky to tackle this time—quite a girl, Miss Golinsky—and you know, that confirms a suspicion in my mind. The only casing he did was looking for female names on the mail slots. If he'd ever laid eyes on Miss Golinsky before he made the attempt on her, he'd never have rung her doorbell."

Piggott laughed. "She sounds like an Amazon."

"I also think he must be a frustrated actor," said Mendoza. "Why, he had a beautiful setup without all that elaborate bedtime story, Matt. All he'd have had to do was show up in his uniform and say he was checking for gas leaks or something. What honest citizen would be afraid of the stalwart young firefighter?"

"Too simple for him. He got some of his kicks out of the approach," said Piggott, who occasionally surprised Mendoza with unexpected imagination.

On Monday morning Higgins and Landers were just leaving the office to hunt more heisters—there hadn't been a lab report on the Eggers house yet, of course, and they had put Fuller in Pending—when Lake beckoned Higgins as they passed the switchboard. "Long distance for you."

Higgins went back to his desk and picked up the phone. "Sergeant Higgins."

"This is Chief Lombard, Stamford P.D.," said a heavy voice in his ear. "You'll be the LAPD man who sent us some prints and a query about Robert Gillespie? Don't tell me you've got him. What for? They're his prints all right. Have you got him?"

"Only," said Higgins, "in a manner of speaking. Why?"

"Because if you've got him we want him. For murder."

"I'll be damned," said Higgins. "Now we know. He's dead," and he told the chief what had happened to Mr. Gillespie.

"That is really one for the books," said Lombard. The distinctive New England accent rang a little strange on Higgins' ear. "We'll never know the whole truth of the matter now, but that winds up one of the queerest cases I've ever had, and I've been on this force for thirty-two years."

"Who did he kill?"

"His wife. He had a hardware store here, just another little humdrum medium-successful businessman. Set your clock by him. Careful of money. Opened the store at nine six days a week, closed at five—had a good many friends around town, he was born and brought up here—member of Rotary and the Masons, went to church every Sunday with his wife. She was the same kind—local girl. They never had a family. She played bridge with other women, gave dinner parties, taught a Sunday-school class. Once a year they went to the Cape for a week on vacation. Married nearly thirty years, never any sign of trouble between them. Then one day eight years ago he closed up the store one Saturday night, went home and shot his wife through the head, buried her in the back yard, packed a couple of bags and vanished."

"I will be goddamned," said Higgins.

"By the time it came to light and we found her—some of her friends wondering why she hadn't come to church, wouldn't answer the phone—the trail was cold. We traced him to New York, and for all the signs there were he might have gone to Timbuctoo, or just rented a room in the Bowery as John Smith. We had flyers out on him for quite a while, had him listed as wanted with NCIC, but we never had a smell of him. The only thing we did know was that he took a bundle of cash with him. Before he went home that day he visited his bank and closed out his whole savings account —had a hell of an argument with the manager because he asked for cash, but he finally got it. The manager thought he was crazy, and then when the store didn't open on Monday —and the ladies got talking—"

"How much did he take?"

"Nearly twenty thousand."

"My God. He had nine hundred left."

"Did he, now. I'd like, by God, to know all of that story, and now we never will," said Lombard regretfully.

"Is there any relative back there who might be due the money?"

"Nary a soul. You'd better use it to bury him, Sergeant. And I'd kind of like a snapshot of the grave as a souvenir."

Hackett came into Mendoza's office just after lunch that Monday and said, "I don't think there's anything to this Rush thing, Luis."

"Just the lady's imagination?"

"And she doesn't like Rush, thinks he treated her niece badly. I still say it'd be a damned silly way to try to kill somebody—you couldn't be sure. More to the point, Rush seems to be all broken up, especially over the little girl, and he's not a genius, I don't think he's putting it on."

"I'll trust you to know. Just the lady's imagination." His phone rang and he picked it up. "Hey," said Lake, "I've got Nick on the line."

"Well, *paisano*," said Mendoza, "welcome back. We've missed you."

"I can't say the same," said Galeano. "But I see we got back ahead of a heat wave, at least. It was nice up in Yosemite— Oh, I walked into that one, you needn't pull the punch line. Anything exciting going on?"

"A few—mmh—peculiar excitements," said Mendoza. "When do we get you back?"

"Well, that's what I called about. I've got six days saved up and Marta wants to spend them house hunting. We figure we'd better buy a place now if we're ever going to, before prices go up any higher. We thought maybe Glendale or Burbank."

"So we struggle along without you for another week. Good luck on it, Nick, but the interest rates—"

"Little you know about interest rates. Oh, say, I saw some of the stories about your politician. Now that girl—quite a luscious piece—of course I only got a glimpse at the picture before Marta took it away from me—" In the background she could be heard denying that vigorously.

"Art's still thinking of taking up a collection for the fellow who inadvertently got him off the June ballot."

"I'll buy that. Well, I'll be with you on Saturday, and hold the good thoughts that we find a nice house."

"A nice big house—you're only thirty-five, Nick." Mendoza put the phone down, laughing.

For once, the lab got on the ball, and a report on the Eggers house came in on Tuesday at one o'clock. Hackett brought it in to show Mendoza the rather horrifying pictures. "They picked up a lot of latents, they're still checking them."

"Yes," said Mendoza, looking at the glossy eight-by-ten prints. "And I'll bet you they don't make any, Art."

"What have you spotted?"

Mendoza grimaced. "The senseless violence. The overkill. Who are the wildest ones around these days? The ones most apt to create this sort of—of bloodbath?"

"Oh, yes," said Hackett, and shut his eyes. "The vicious kids."

"*Exactamente.* Whose prints we don't have on file." The phone rang and he picked it up.

"Somebody for Art," said Lake.

Hackett took the phone from Mendoza. "This is Sergeant Hackett."

"Oh!" said a female voice. "Mrs. Bickerstaff said you

wanted to ask me some questions. This is Alice McLennan."

"Oh, yes, Miss McLennan, I could come to see you now if—"

"Oh, I have to go right past the police building on my way to work, I got a new job yesterday at a drugstore on Hill Street. I'll be glad to stop by."

When she got there, Hackett and Palliser ushered her into Mendoza's office. Alice McLennan was a large-framed woman with brown hair, a pleasant rather pretty face, blue eyes behind crystal glasses. She took the chair Mendoza offered her. She looked at them and said, "I was never so surprised in my life when I heard about Mr. Parmenter, when I got home on Saturday. And I'm sorry to sound un-Christian, but he deserved murdering! But what did you want to ask me? I wouldn't know a thing about it, I wasn't even here."

"Well, you see," said Mendoza, "we were just a little curious, Miss McLennan. About why you quit your job with him. You told Mrs. Bickerstaff it was because he was the wickedest man in the world. Why?"

She sat up straight and her mouth drew tight. "It was because of what I found out about him that day," she said, and her voice was angry. "He was a queer man, he never talked much, and he was mostly sitting in the stockroom writing, scribbling away like mad, I never knew at what. He only waited on the prescription counter, I did everything else." So Parmenter had composed some of the hate literature. "But that day, it was March nineteenth, he was mixing up something in the dispensing room, and I went to ask him if it was Mrs. Alford's prescription because she'd just called to ask whether it was ready—and he said no, it wasn't—his eyes looked awfully glittery and queer—he said this was for old Weekes' damned tomcat—he said he'd cleared most of the damned animals out—everybody who lived around him was animal-crazy, he said—and they came spoiling his garden, he hated them all, and he'd gotten all of them except this damned cat, and there was enough strychnine in this brew to kill a dozen. Oh, it was the most horrible, horrible—he said it in an awful kind of gloating way—how he'd poisoned the Hilbrands' yappy little mutt, and that big brute of the Sadlers', and that mangy hound of the Andersons' and all the damned cats came digging up his garden, there was just one left and he was going to get it yet— Oh, I was absolutely horrified!" Her eyes flashed fire. "Anyone who would poison an animal would poison a child—a person—and the cruelty of it—I just couldn't stand to be around such a man, and I quit on the spot right then—"

"I don't blame you," said Hackett. "I agree with you, Miss McLennan."

"And even if I turned him in to the police, it's only a fine, he wouldn't go to jail—"

"It's a misdemeanor," said Mendoza, and his eyes were very cold. "I don't know what the current fine is—and the legal worth of the animal thrown in, which is damned nonsense."

"Oh, it upset me so dreadfully," she said, getting out a handkerchief to wipe her eyes. "I kept worrying and worrying about it, I couldn't sleep—you see, I kept thinking, suppose those people got other pets, not knowing there was such an evil man right in their midst, and he did it again!—because he would have—I thought about it a whole week, and I finally decided, before Mickey and I went on vacation, I had to warn them. I knew where he lived because of the emergency sign on the door. I'd never been there before, such a funny little street—"

"Who did you talk to?" asked Hackett.

"I saw the Hilbrands next door to him, that Saturday afternoon. And they thanked me over and over for coming—she cried and said they'd lost the dearest little dog—dying in convulsions, and the children saw it, oh, it's too dreadful to think about—and there'd been the Branagans' old spaniel, and the Andersons had just worshiped their Labrador—everyone on the street had lost a pet—she said Miss Spooner had the most beautiful Siamese cat— Oh, I can't bear to think of such wickedness! Well, that was why I quit the job—if that's all you wanted to know. And"—looking at her watch, wiping her eyes a last time—"if I'm going to find a parking place I'd better get on. If that's all you wanted to know." She went to the door, and turned to add a parting shot. "I hope you never find out who killed him! Whoever did it deserves a medal!"

They sat looking at each other, and suddenly Hackett began to laugh. He bent over, laughing helplessly, and he gasped, "Don't you—see it? Don't you see—it's—it's the *Orient Express!*" And Palliser began to laugh too. "They all—knew about it—everybody on that street—they were all in on it! That day! Oh, my God, that day we were there, John—when I think— Oh, my God! I'll bet you, I just bet you—they all got together, talked it over and decided—oh, my God—on the vigorous action. The necessary beating up. Oh, my *dear* God, when I think— They all had such sweet reasonable excuses why they hadn't seen or heard a thing. Not a thing, Officer." He was rocking back and forth with deadly mirth. "The Klabers watching TV—and the Kellers painting the back bedroom—"

Palliser wiped his eyes. "Those Andersons refinishing furniture, and the people kept awake by the baby—"

"Mrs. Hilbrand and her sinus headache—"

"But it was him," said Palliser, ignoring grammar in inspiration. "It was him—the cabdriver with all the muscles—"

"Oh, no, no, John!" gasped Hackett. "No, it was that simple innocent big Irishman Branagan! It had to be Branagan—him bushed on a Sunday, dozing in front of the TV! And I'll tell you something else, they got the children out of the way so they wouldn't see it—Hilbrand took theirs to the zoo, and Mrs. Branagan took hers to her mother's. And I'll bet Mrs. Hilbrand stayed home to act as a lookout while Branagan administered the earned beating— Oh, my God, I *knew* there was something funny about that street that day!"

"*¡Qué bello—hermoso!*" Mendoza was grinning like a happy wolf. "And you know something else beautiful, boys? We'll never get anybody for it, because there's no evidence at all."

"No, of course not," said Palliser, "and nobody meant the man to be killed. I must say it isn't going to worry me at all."

"Maybe," said Hackett, still giggling, "we ought to get up an anonymous collection for Branagan—"

"All I can say is," said Mendoza, "they must be a bunch of natural actors, such a beautiful job of covering up—and I'm not going to lose any sleep over it either. Mr. Parmenter was distinctly no loss to the human race."

He drove home that night ruminating on that and various things—Alison would enjoy the story—on the Eggerses, and on Rush—could he be another natural actor? When he came around the last curve at the top of Hamlin Place, he braked sharply to avoid a black-and-white Burbank squad car slewed across the street. There were, all told, three squad cars, here in front of the half dozen houses at the top of this highest street in Burbank—and all five of the sheep, busily eating bushes and lawns. The uniformed men were standing in the street, and there were householders out all over.

"Where the hell did any sheep come from in the middle of town, Tom?"

"Oh, oh, it's eating my azaleas—oh, get it *out*—"

"And what the hell are we going to do about it, Barney?"

"Oh, they're ruining all my hibiscus—can't you do something?"

Those damned young devils fooling with the gate again, thought Mendoza. He got out, claimed the sheep, offered reparations, said if they'd let him past he would send a man down to round them up. He shot up the rest of the hill reflecting that that pair of young hellions were too much like their mother, damn it, and spoiled into the bargain, and something would have to be done about it.

The gates, of course, were slightly ajar, as the twins had left them. He pushed the gadget on the dashboard and the gates swung open. He gunned the engine, and the gates swung smartly forward and smashed in the radiator and front bumper of the Ferrari with a resounding clang.

He was still sitting there swearing when everybody came running down to investigate the crash.